# Contest Queen

Acclaimed Contest Queen Carol Shaffer shares her fascinating story and How-To secrets for winning contests and sweepstakes.

### By Carol Shaffer

# CONTEST QUEEN
## Acclaimed Contest Queen Carol Shaffer shares her fascinating story and How-To secrets for winning contests and sweepstakes

## Copyright 2002 by Carol Shaffer

ISBN 0-9663393-8-X
Library of Congress 2002103459
First Edition, 2002

Published by Truman Publishing Company
Printed in the United States of America

Editing and Book Layout by James D. Criswell
Chapter Title Illustrations by Althea Hofmaier

All correspondence and credit card orders contact:

Truman Publishing Company
218 Delaware, Suite #303, Kansas City, MO 64105
Or call toll free: 1-888-852-3694
**www.trumanpublishing.com**

# Dedication

This book is dedicated to my mother, Wilma Wright, for giving me the confidence to follow my dreams, and to Edward Reinbold, my friend and advisor, whose collaboration helped to make this book possible.

It is also dedicated to my extraordinary and remarkable children, Donna, Diana, and Donald and to my sons-in-law Jim and Mark and to my daughter-in-law Debra. Thank you for the precious gifts in my life, my grandchildren; Amanda, Jimmy, Ryan, Hannah, Alynn, David, Caroline, and Drew. May joy smile on you all and bless you forever!

A special thank you goes to my sister, Jo Ann, and brother-in-law Bob, for their encouragement and undying faith in all my endeavors. Thank you also to Jim Criswell of Truman Publishing for publishing this book and to Adam Crosley for producing my "Win Big" video.

# Table of Contents

## Chapter 4: Be Creative!
## The Key to Winning

## Chapter 5: Spot the Rainbow &
## Find the Pot of Gold!
### Sources for Contesting

## Chapter 6: Creating the Winning Entry
## Imagination Is the Key!

## Chapter 7: Participation Contests
## Showcase Your Talent!

# Chapter 8:  TV Game Shows
## Your Chance To Be a Star!

# Chapter 9:  You're Never Too Old,
## or Too Young!
### Contesting for children

# Chapter 10:  Contesting In the
## New Millennium!
### Making the Internet Payoff

# Chapter 11: Watching Your P's and Q's

# Chapter 12: Pageants, Powder & Potpourri
## Be alert & imaginative to win

# Foreword

Welcome to the exciting, sometimes lucrative and sometimes glamorous world of contesting and sweepstaking. Some people say am I just plain "lucky", but "luck" is not the reason that I have won approximately $150,000.00 in prizes over the last seven years. I have developed a system of techniques and strategies that I use to increase my odds of winning, and I share those techniques and strategies with you in this book. You can use these tactics to increase your chances of winning some great prizes too. Somebody has to win and it may as well be you or me. You won't win every contest or sweepstake that you enter, I don't, but hopefully you will win a number of them. The first time I tried one of my strategies I was surprised to learn that I had won a $10,000.00 shopping spree. I couldn't believe how easy it was! I proceeded to enter more contests and sweepstakes and won even more fabulous prizes while creating a new hobby for myself that I thoroughly enjoy. I hope you find my avocation as much fun and as rewarding as I have.

--- Carol Shaffer

CAROL'S WORLD

## Chapter 1

# Welcome to the Wonderful World of Winning!

---

**In This Chapter**

➤ What exactly is "*Contesting*"?

➤ Fun for the whole family

➤ Anyone can do it!

➤ A little bit about Carol.

➤ Enjoy a glamorous lifestyle!

➤ Become a celebrity yourself!

➤ Contesting as an opportunity to help others

---

*When you wish upon a star it makes no difference who you are.*
No truer words were ever written when it comes to the
fascinating and often rewarding hobby of *Contesting*.

If you're like most people, you probably never thought of
contesting as a hobby. Chances are the idea never even crossed
your mind, but it's been my hobby for several years now and I've
discovered that it's a lot of fun and you will be amazed when I tell
you about all of the wonderful prizes that I've won.

It still amazes and astounds me every time I win something, whether it's a big prize or something of lesser value. I jokingly tell my friends that if a goat was offered as a prize I would try to win it! I just love winning, and to date, I have won close to $150,000 in prizes for myself, my relatives, and for my friends.

I don't win every contest that I enter, not by a long shot, but in a surprisingly high percentage of them I do win something. By my estimate I've entered around 1,000 contests and I've won over 100 times. I think you'll agree that a 10% win rate is far better than pure chance. In fact, chance or luck really has very little to do with it.

I won a $10,000 shopping spree at an upscale regional mall. My husband won a brand new $30,000 car. I've won trips to San Francisco, San Antonio, and Hawaii. My daughter and I took a virtually all expense paid trip to Australia to see the Olympics compliments of Coca-Cola.

These big wins are just some of the highlights of my contesting career. I've won numerous small prizes, fun prizes, so have many of my friends and family using the techniques revealed in this book. For me, winning is always fun, whether the prizes is a diamond or a donut. It's always a thrill to pick up the phone or open the mail and hear or read, "Congratulations! You're a Winner!"

## What exactly is "Contesting"

The Watchwords Are:

*Be Alert!*
and
*Be Creative!*

"Contesting", as I use the word, is a pastime and an avocation that involves an organized approach to entering and winning contests, sweepstakes, games, game shows, and pageants. Unlike the vast majority of people who may casually drop their name in the box for a prize drawing once in a while, or occasionally send in a sweepstakes entry, the contest hobbyist is *organized* and has a *strategy* for winning.

The devoted Contester is constantly on the *alert* for new opportunities to win, just as a coin or stamp collector must be watchful for a new chance to further their collection, or a hunter must be on the lookout for game.

A successful Contester must also be *creative*. As I will explain, creativity is really the key to winning more than your fair share of the contests that you enter.

Those are the two watchwords of contesting—be **_alert_** and be **_creative_**!

## Contesting is inexpensive

Unlike a lot of hobbies contesting is inexpensive. There's no special equipment to buy. You don't have to invest hundreds of dollars as you might if you took up woodworking, golfing, hunting, fishing, or many other hobbies.

## Devote just as much time as you like

You don't have to devote a lot of time to the hobby to enjoy it and profit from it. Like any other hobby it takes a little study and practice, but you can give it just as much time and attention as you like. Of course the more contests that you enter and the more of my techniques that you study and employ the greater your reward is likely to be.

## Fun for the whole family

One of the most fun things about contesting for me is that it can involve the whole family. It didn't take very

> **Kids Learn While They Have Fun!**
> Many kid's contests are educational; like essay contests and art contests.

long at all after I took up contesting as a hobby before my family started to notice how much fun I was having—and how many prizes I was winning.

Now it's a family affair! My daughters and sons-in-law, son and daughter-in-law, my gentleman friend Ed, my nieces and nephews, even my grandchildren—we're all Contesters. We're all having a ball together and we're winning *fabulous* prizes.

Can you imagine how much fun it is to strategize with your little granddaughter about her contest entry, to sit down at the kitchen table and help her prepare her entry, and then get to see her big smile when she finds out that she won?

You're never to young to win contests. For example when my two and a half year old grandson David won the Elmo Contest he helped with the contest by sticking Sesame Stickers on his entry. Before that, he won a go-cart when he was only one year old!

I think I get a bigger kick out of seeing one of my grandkids win a contest than winning myself. And, yes, there are lots of contests out there for children and I'm going to tell you about a few.

## Anyone can do it!

Polo is the pastime of the idol rich. Some people think that stamp collecting is for eggheads. Needlework, for some reason, seems to appeal more to the ladies than to the men. Golfing requires both time and money, and most of us are short on both. The same thing goes for snow skiing. *Contesting, however, is for everybody!*

You don't have to have much money. You don't have to be real smart. You don't have to travel and, unlike what you may be thinking, you don't have to be lucky. With the tips I'm going to share with you the harder you work at contesting the luckier you'll be! Contesting can even be a good hobby for shut-ins or handicapped people.

**4**

# I'm what you'd call "A regular gal".

Over the last five or six years that I've been an active Contester I've won prizes valued at around $150,000 **altogether— in cash,** merchandise, and trips. That's right—one hundred and fifty thousand dollars! And believe me, I'm just a regular work-a-day type of person, just like most of us.

A lady doesn't have to tell how old she is, but I will tell you that I didn't even start seriously contesting until I was in my late fifties. I'm a mother of three, a son and two daughters. They're all grown up now and I've been blessed with eight beautiful grandkids.

I live in Columbia, Illinois in suburban St. Louis. Most of my life has been centered around taking care of my family. I did write a column for the local newspaper at one time. I was a Girl Scout leader, at the age of 53. I belong to the Columbia Woman's Club and to the American Legion Post Auxiliary. After the girls were grown I'm proud to say that I went back to college and finally got a degree at a rather ripe old age.

My ex-husband and I got married too young I guess, it's a pretty typical story these days. We drifted apart over the years. Well, anyway, we're no longer married—and that's enough on that subject. I only bring it up to avoid the possibility of confusing the reader. You will notice that sometimes in this book I refer to "My Husband" and prizes that we won while we were married. Other times I refer to "My Gentleman Friend" and the prizes that we have won.

After my divorce I took a job at our local WalMart. A girl's got to have health insurance and WalMart is really a pretty good place to work. (I hope my boss is reading this.) They let me work evenings so I can devote my days to contesting, and that suits me just fine.

So you see, I'm just your average Jane. There's nothing all that special about little old Carol Shaffer. If I can do it, so can you! That's why I decided to write this book, so everybody can share in the fun and excitement that I have enjoyed since I got serious about contesting.

## Why not enjoy a glamorous lifestyle! After all, you deserve it!

I've had so many, many, opportunities for fun and excitement because of my contesting that honestly I cannot imagine how much different my life might have been if I'd never gotten into it. After all, I'm just a regular gal from a little town in Illinois, but because of my contesting I've had the opportunity to experience so much more that life has to offer.

> **I've had so many, many, opportunites for fun and excitement because of my contesting!**

I've been able to travel all over the United States. Not only that but I've literally become a world traveler, that's something that I know never would have happened without my contesting.

For instance, when one of my entries won a trip to the 1999 Super Bowl in Miami, Florida for my friend Ed we had the option of accepting $4,000 instead. That's unusual, most of the time a sweepstakes sponsor does not give you that option. We took the cash and used it to tour all of the Scandinavian countries.

We visited the capital cities and saw the "The Little Mermaid" in Denmark. We also visited St. Petersburg, Russia's cultural capital. My son is a firefighter and collects fireman's patches. I try to pick up patches for him where ever I travel. A firefighter captain in St. Petersburg tore a fire patch right off of his uniform to give to me. He also gave us Russian calendars, playing cards, and photos of the fire station, along with some Russion medallions.

Now I ask you, when was the last time you had to decide whether you'd rather go to the Super Bowl or to take a trip to Europe? It doesn't happen to most of us very often does it. But it happened to me because of my contesting.

Thanks to contesting I've had the opportunity to meet and chat with lots of famous celebrities. I've met movie stars, sports heroes, and TV and radio personalities, all because of contesting.

Did Miss America ever visit your house? Because of contesting I had the opportunity to meet Debbye Turner, a former Miss America. When one of the St. Louis TV stations decided to do a segment about my hobby Debbye Turner came to my house to do the interview. I remember seeing Debbye on television the night that she was crowned Miss America. I was so thrilled to get to meet her in person.

At the time of her reign as Miss America she'd been studying veterinarian science at the University of Missouri. It was obvious that she likes animals. She petted my cat George and spoke affectionately about her two cats. I can see why Debbye won the Miss America Pageant. She is truly a beautiful person, inside and out.

## You might even become a celebrity yourself!

Not only do you get to meet celebrities because of winning contests and sweepstakes but one of the perks of the hobby is that you are sometimes treated like a celebrity yourself. This aspect of the hobby might not appeal to everyone, but I get a big kick out of it.

After you appear on a local TV show, or have an article about you published in a newspaper or magazine, people may start to recognize you on the street. I think it's fun and interesting to do television and radio shows. I like seeing first hand just how broadcasting works.

I've had articles, with photos, about my contesting experiences published in *Good Housekeeping, Woman's World, The National Enquirer, The National Examiner, The St. Louis Post-Dispatch, The Belleville News Democrat* (that was a feature on the cover of the Sunday magazine insert), *The Suburban Journal,* and *The Columbia Clarion.*

I have been interviewed on ABC World News from New York, KMOV Channel 4, Pertzborn's People, The "Show Me St. Louis Show", Fox News, Channel 5 KSD-TV, Channel 30 news, and Channel 46 "At Your Service Show". I have been interviewed on radio stations in almost every state in the U.S.A and as far away as New Zealand.

And just think...It Could All Happen to You!

## An opportunity to help others

One of the most satisfying things about my hobby to me is that it gives me the opportunity to help my family members and others. My contesting has positively enriched the lives of my entire family, and that makes me feel good. Everyone in my family has been able to take trips and enjoy owning various material things that they never would have bought for themselves, sometimes things that they never would have been able to buy for themselves.

On those occasions where I've won several of the same prizes, like the time when I won seven television sets, I try to use the windfall to help others. I gave one of the televisions to a man whose television was broken, and he didn't have the funds to get it repaired or buy a new one. I gave another television to my sister and her husband after their set was stolen. I offered another television to a teen center to use as a raffle prize. After I won a $10,000 shopping spree I received a letter suggesting that I buy some new clothes of a sick child. I probably would have done that, except the person who sent me the letter forgot to sign it.

## Chapter 2

# So Many Contests So Little Time!

**In This Chapter**
➤ Contesting is nothing new
➤ Contests and Sweepstakes are everywhere
➤ Where do you begin

## Contesting is nothing new

Contesting is nothing new, it's been with us throughout history. Remember the Knights of Old? They held participation contests called jousting, a test of horsemanship, and bravery. The prize was that the winning team would hold the losers for ransom.

According to Encyclopedia Britannica French towns were holding lotteries to raise money for defense way back in the 1400s. Florence, Italy held a municipal lottery in 1530. Queen Elizabeth the First held a little state lottery in England in 1567— they sold 400,000 tickets. A lottery helped raise money to settle Jamestown, Virginia in 1612.

There was an interesting raffle held in St. Joseph, Missouri during the Civil War. The Patee House in old St. Joe was possibly the finest hotel west of the Mississippi at the time. It's owner, John Patee, was a backer of the Confederacy. When Union troops took over and occupied the hotel he decided to sell it in a nation-wide raffle. April 28, 1865 was the announced date for the drawing however 100 tickets remained unsold so John Patee bought them himself. And guess what? He won his own hotel back.

## Contests and sweepstakes are everywhere

I guess contests and sweepstakes must have been around ever since Adam was nibbling on that apple that Eve handed to him. Today there are literally thousands of contests and sweepstakes to pick from. You can certainly find a few to fit your talents and interests.

There are fishing contests, trivia contests, and contests for amateur radio buffs. There are contests for art, poetry (including haiku), recipes, cooking, writing, storytelling, and coloring contests for the kids. There are cute baby contests, and photography contests, pie eating contests, and pie baking contests. You name it and we human beings seem to try to figure a way to make a contest out of it.

> **Did you know that there is a "Painted Pottie" contest?**
> Uh-huh, checkout www.paintedpotties.com

We're now all traveling on the "information highway" and mankind has taken our passion for contests right into the Internet age. Using the Alta Vista search engine I found that there are 380,642 web sites listing the word *"sweepstakes"*. But that's nothing, there are 2,115,228 web sites that contain the word *"contest"*.

You're riding in your car and you find that every radio station on the dial is having some kind of contest. Turn on the TV and it's the same thing. Go to the mall, the supermarket, the hardware store, or the fast food joint and you'll find a contest or drawing. Ed McMann and Dick Clark are cruising up and down our neighborhood streets trying to find their million dollar winners.

## Where do you begin?

The trick for the serious contester isn't to find a contest—they're everywhere! The trick is knowing one contest from another and carefully choosing which ones to enter. You can't enter them all, that's ridiculous, you don't have the time and if you did you couldn't afford the stamps! Consequently it's important to be selective and to devote your limited time and efforts to exactly the right contests or sweepstakes.

This doesn't mean that you want to limit yourself to trying to win just one particular contest or sweepstakes. Naturally you increase your chances of winning by entering a lot of different contests. What you want to do is limit yourself to those that meet the criteria that you establish for yourself in targeting your efforts, and I'll get to some of those criteria shortly.

## Chapter 3

# Let's Get Organized Just For the Fun of It!

---

**In This Chapter**

➤ Contesting is serious business
➤ Organize your workspace
➤ Organize your supplies
➤ Organize your strategies
➤ Plan your budget

---

## "Contesting" as a hobby is serious business

Yes, contesting is fun but just like anything else planning and organization will be an important part of your success. Once you take up the hobby of contesting you leave behind the ranks of those mere ordinary people who enter a contest here and there, once in a while, without much hope or expectation of winning. You expect to win! And you are going to win! Part of your edge is that you take the whole thing rather seriously and take an organized approach with your efforts.

## Organize your workspace

The first step in organization is to get your work place and tools in order. Artists have their studio lofts and woodworkers have their workshop, likewise a serious contester designs a workspace suited to the hobby.

You'll need a place to fill out all of those entry blanks, and postcards. If you have the space in your house to set up a small contesting office that's ideal. If not, that's OK there's no rule against working from your kitchen table.

You'll need a little filing space because you will want to keep track of the contests that you've entered. Often you'll also want to keep a record of the techniques that you used when entering a particular contest so that you can refer to your notes the next time a similar contest roles around. Every time that you enter a contest you'll want to file a copy of the entry blank in case you later need to refer to the official rules.

You'll also need a little space to store your contesting supplies so you'll have them readily on hand. If you're sitting down to write out 30 entry postcards so that you can send in a contest entry

> **A place for everything, and everything in its place.**
> *Benjamin Franklin*

everyday for a month you don't want to have to spend extra time hunting for your pen, postcards, or stamps.

Simply stated, your contesting workspace should be organized just as efficiently as any business office. It's not a business, but if your serious you are going to be working at it as if it were. You need a quiet, orderly, place to work so you can concentrate your time and effort on sending in those winning entries.

## Organize your supplies

There are a few tools of the contesting trade that you'll want to keep on hand for the sake of efficiency. If the reasoning behind some of these supply items is unclear to you, don't worry, we'll get to the explanation.

Here's a peak into my supply drawer.

- An assortment of pens and markers. Use indelible ink so your writing won't smear.

- Colorful envelopes and stationary. It might be stationary or envelopes with balloons, animals, flowers, etc. on them. This in addition to a supply of plain white stationary and envelopes.

- Three by five inch index cards. If you are out of a contest's entry blanks sponsors usually allow these as substitute entry blanks.

> **Contesting workspace should be organized just as efficienntly as any business office.**

- Postcards, both plain and pre-stamped ones from the post office and an assortment of picture postcards.

- An assortment of colored markets and pens, including various color bingo markers.

- A magnifying glass to read the rules. Contest rules are often in fine, hard to read, print.

- Pinking shears.

- Stamps. Always buy the self-adhesive, non-lick kind.

With a little creativity (there's that watch word again) you can stock your supply drawers without spending a lot of money.

We save colorful envelopes from birthday cards. I regularly check with stationery or card shops. Sometimes they have inventory that they want to get rid of a little or no cost. I also check with friends for left over envelopes from Christmas cards that they don't want.

Picture post cards are great for entering contests and sweepstakes because the cards are colorful and stand out and they are the right size for most rule stipulations. You don't always have to buy picture post cards, sometimes companies offer free post cards especially at hotels and motels.

I even make my own envelopes sometimes. I use a regular #10 envelope as a pattern and make colorful, eye-catching, enclosures from heavy wrapping paper, stationary, or even wallpaper.

## Organize your strategy

As I mentioned previously you couldn't enter every contest that you run across, it would be foolish to even think of trying. You'll want to give some thought to the kind of contest or sweepstakes that most appeal to you, and plan to specialize in those.

You'll need to decide whether you prefer to play contests or sweepstakes, or maybe you're like me and you decide to pick and choose a few of each. Without getting too technical or running for the dictionary let me explain the difference between a contest and a sweepstakes.

A contest requires that you do something that is judged against the other contestant entries. Write an essay, for instance, sing a song, create a costume, come up with a recipe, or any of a thousand other activities that contest sponsors dream up.

A sweepstakes, on the other hand, is a random drawing. It could be a national sweepstakes with entries coming in from all over the country. It could be a regional sweepstakes conducted by a company that only operates in a particular part of the country.

**15**

Or it could be a simple drop the entry in the box in-store drawing to win a free pizza at your neighborhood pizza place.

I like to enter both contests and sweepstakes. Many times I get a big kick out of the activity that a contest requires. I like to write, and dress up in costume, and think up creative ways to make my contest entry the winner.

I've found that contests or sweepstakes that have a short deadline offer a better chance for success. If the contest will not be going on for very long, chances are fewer people will have entered.

I find that during vacation and Christmas time people are generally busier and don't take the time to enter as many contests. If the sweepstakes or contest rules list some states where residents can't enter that's good because it means there will be that many less entries.

> **Contests or sweepstakes that have a short deadline offer a better chance of winning.**

When the cost of stamps increases people may cut back on postage spending and not enter as often. Once I read an article about a woman who sold her blood to get money for contesting stamps. I haven't gone that far yet, but stamps can be costly.

Many people like to try to win radio call-in contests. I have a friend that has an extra telephone line in his house specifically for radio call-in's. He has more than one radio playing at the same time so he can monitor his opportunities. I don't do the radio contests myself because I am not often home standing by the phone.

One word of caution about radio call-in contests; the radio stations don't like to have the same people calling in all of the time and winning all of their contests. After all, they're not sponsoring the contest because they just like to give things away. They want to attract listeners with their promotions and they like to spread the prizes around throughout the area. If you call a

**16**

particular radio station too often they may decide that you are what they call a "Contest Pig" and ban you from calling.

## Plan your budget

Contesting is a fun hobby but you need to remember that that's what it is—a hobby. You don't want to get carried away. Decide in advance how much of your hard earned money you want to spend on contesting and stick to it.

To me, thinking up creative ways to economize on my contesting supplies is part of the fun. Personally I budget only five dollars a week for stamps and other supplies and I've found that I can have all of the fun I can handle without busting the budget.

## Chapter 4

# Be Creative!
# The Key
# To Winning

## In This Chapter
➤ Think positive
➤ Have a creative mind and use your imagination
➤ What judges look for
➤ Biggest mistake most people make

## Think Positive

One important difference between you as a contest hobbiest and your competition (the rest of the folks entering the same contest) is that you **expect** to win. Don't underestimate that advantage. The first step toward succeeding at anything is to believe that you can succeed and contesting is no different. I don't know how many times I've heard someone say, "Oh, I don't enter many contests, I never win anything anyway." I'm sure you've heard people say the same thing, maybe you've even said it yourself.

Well starting today you are going to rid yourself of that negative thinking. You ARE going to win! There's no question about it. If you follow a few of the suggestions in this book and put in a little bit of time and effort you are going to be simply amazed at how much fun you can have and how many contests and sweepstakes you can win.

# Have a creative mind
# and use your imagination.

A simple technique that hardly any of your competition ever puts into use is to do something to make your entry standout in the bin. The individual selecting the winning entry blank does not intentional play a favorite but still, if one entry blank is more colorful, or if it is stiffer or fan folded to take up a little more room among the entries than it has a better chance of being the entry blank that's fished out as the winner.

Instead of an entry blank, for instance, I sometimes use the label or the box top of sponsoring company as my entry blank. This way the sponsor knows I use the product and hopefully help to get my entry chosen. This technique also saves me the cost of index cards or post cards.

> **You Have To Have a GIMMICK!**
> **Do something, anything, that causes your entry to standout!**

Sometimes I will decorate my entry with an appropriate picture cut out from a magazine. For example I might glue a cut-out of a ship on an entry to try to win a cruise, or a cut-out of a Dutch windmill to try to win a trip to Holland. Decorating entries can be a fun pass time to do with your children, on in my case, my grandchildren.

You have to have a gimmick! Do something—anything—that causes your entry to standout from the rest. Be creative and you'll think of lots of ways to make your entry a little different and maybe a little more attention getting.

Your strategy doesn't have to be complicated or even particularly time consuming. For instance, one time I saw an ad in the Sunday newspaper supplement announcing that a particular chain of tile stores was sponsoring an in-store drawing for a trip to Hawaii. My son Donald and his fiancee Debbie were planning to be married soon and I thought a trip to Hawaii would make a perfect honeymoon.

I went to as many different locations as I could find of this particular tile store and entered both their names. My strategy was relatively simple. I filled out the blanks with different colored magic markers.

By the time the winner was announced Donald and Debbie were already married. They'd purchased and were in the process of redecorating their first house. Unfortunately they didn't win the Grand Prize trip to Hawaii, but they were delighted to learn that they won First Prize; a $1,500 gift certificate for floor tile. It was perfect timing for them. They were able to put beautiful ceramic tile in their kitchen and had enough buying power left over to do one bathroom in marble.

The colored magic marker strategy didn't require any extra time or effort at all. You certainly wouldn't have to be a genius to think of it but it did get the desired results. My advise is do anything that you can think of that makes your entry a little bit different from all of the others. It works!

## What judges look for

Contest judges are people and like the rest of us they are influenced by their perceptions. If they see one entry blank among all of the others that is more colorful than the others they are naturally drawn to it. A newspaper advertising salesperson will tell you that a color ad is 60% to 80% more effective than a black and white ad. There's a reason for this—people notice color. **Color gets results.**

Sometimes I think a judge reaches for one of my colorful entry blanks simply out of curiosity. He or she is curious to see the picture that I've pasted on the entry blank, or they are wondering who in the world would think of sending in a fluorescent pink entry.

The other thing that judges look for is neatness. When it comes to contesting—*neatness counts!* A judge isn't going to work very much to read your entry. Why should he? If the first entry blank that comes out of the hopper is difficult to read there are plenty more to chose from.

I try not to fill out so many entry blanks at one sitting that I get writer's cramp, after all this is supposed to be a fun hobby. It partially defeats the purpose if you make it too much like work. I take entry forms with me if I have to go to the dentist or doctor, or anywhere that I have a long wait, I simply fill out the entry blanks while I'm waiting.

> **Judges look for COLOR, NEATNESS, and DID YOU FOLLOW THE RULES!**

I utilize any spare time to fill out the blanks but I concentrate as much on neatness as on speed. It won't do a bit of good if my entry is picked and then put aside because they can't quite read my name or address.

There's a third thing that judges look for and it's very important, which brings me to the next topic.

## Biggest mistakes most people make when entering a contest

The biggest mistake that most people make is so simple that it's obvious—they fail to carefully follow the rules. Why, you might ask yourself, would some one go to the trouble of entering a contest that they have absolutely zero chance of winning? I don't know the answer to that one except to observe that there are a lot of lazy people out there who don't take the time and trouble to read the rules.

If the contest rules say that you can only enter once, then you can only enter once, it's that simple. There's hardly ever a rule though against entering all of your family and friends, and it's loads of fun to spread the winning around.

I always enter my children's names and my friend's name in contests and sweepstakes, especially if the rules allow only one entry per person. I try to let them know that I have entered them so they will be prepared when they get the word that they've won a prize.

Most contest rules prohibit mechanically reproduced entries, so don't do it. If you want to submit multiple entries and there aren't any more entry blanks available sponsors usually allow a three by five inch index card as a substitute entry blank. You can also write to the sponsor of a contest and request an entry form.

**You Can Not Win If You Do Not Follow The Rules!**

When the rules state that you can enter as often as you wish, but each entry must be mailed separately, don't put more than one entry in an envelope. If you do your entries will most likely be disqualified, and if you are disqualified there isn't anything you can do about it. Judges decisions are final.

If I am going to enter a contest or sweepstakes everyday because the rules say one entry per person per day I bring a tablet of entries home with me. When I have time I fill out several blanks and put them into the envelopes and address the envelopes so they are ready to go.

Sometimes the rules call for you to do a little legwork. Do it because lots of people don't bother and they might as well not even enter in the first place.

I won the "Ailse of Discovery Sweepstakes" that was sponsored by *Midwest Living* magazine. The prize was a trip to Hawaii for four people. I was thrilled.

This sweepstakes required the participate to answer a series of questions about various grocery store products. You had to take the entry blank and walk around the store, find a product mentioned on the blank, and answer a specific question about the product. I noticed that the other entries in the entry box had people's names and addresses filled in, but not the answers to the product questions. I knew these entries would be disqualified so I took the time (about 30 minutes) to answer the questions and then dropped my entry into the entry box.

A month later I received a certified letter letting me know that I had won. It was a trip to Hawaii for four people, to the island of your choice. It included airfare, resort accommodations, rental car, a $900 set of golf clubs, and green fees. (Golfing can be quite expensive in Hawaii you know.) All I had to do was decide who to take with me and sign an affidavit of eligibility.

I decided to take my husband and our good friends Wayne and Martha Berry. Martha was battling breast cancer and had always wanted to visit Hawaii. We all agreed that Maui was the island that we'd all like to visit, and it was truly a paradise. We toured the island, went whale watching, went to a luau at the old town of Lahaina. We even took a helicopter ride so we could view Maui from the sky. We went in January when the temperatures back home were below zero. The temperature in Maui was in the 70's.

Another point to be made about following the rules is to be sure and fill out the entry form completely. For instance, if the entry blank asks for a day and evening telephone number be sure and give both. They've called me as early as 7 A.M. in the morning and as late as 10 P.M. in the evening to let me know that I've won again.

## Chapter 5

# Spot the Rainbow
# Find a Pot of Gold!
## Sources for Contesting

---

**In This Chapter**

➤ Contesting Newsletters
➤ Internet Web Sites
➤ Contesting Clubs
➤ Stop, Look and Listen

---

## Use your eagle eyes

People often ask me, "Carol, how do you even find out about all of these contests that you end up winning?" My answer is, "I just keep my eyes open."

The truth is that there is a world of resources out there for contesting, if you know where to look. There are contesting clubs through out the United States. These folks meet regularly to make a party out of their hobby. There are newsletters that you can subscribe to, many of them are even free.

There are dozens, maybe even hundreds, of web sites on the Internet devoted to contests and sweepstakes. Heck, if you've got a computer and Internet access there are an almost unlimited number of contests and sweepstakes that you can enter right from your keyboard.

# Contesting Newsletters

Contesting newsletters are a great way to keep up to date on the hobby. There are monthly publications, weekly publications, and even on-line newsletters that are updated daily. Most of the on-line newsletters are available free of charge since there's no postage or printing expense, all you have to do is sign up.

The weekly publications might give you a slight edge. Because they publish weekly they may include more current and up to date information than the monthly. You have to pay to get the latest updates however. Weekly newsletters are about three times as expensive as the monthly newsletters.

> **Contesting newsletters are great way to keep up to date on the hobby!**

Here's a partial list of available newsletters, along with contact information. There are many, many, other newsletters available, this is merely a representative list. Check out one or more of them and I'm sure you'll find one that's to your liking.

Best Publications
P. O. Box 421163, Plymouth, MN 55442
Fax/Voice Mail (763) 542-0991
E-mail: info@bestsweepstakes.com
http://www.bestsweepstakes.com/bestweekly.html

Playle's Sweepstakes Newsletters
P. O. Box 3051, Des Moines, IA 50316
Fax/Phone (515) 265-2109
E-mail: david@playle.com
http://www.playle.com/psw/index.html

Rags To Riches Sweepstakes Newsletter
P.O. Box 891, Derry, NH 03038
Fax 603-437-3357
E-mail: help@ragstoriches.com
http://www.ragstoriches.com/

SweepsSheet
262 Hawthorn #329wb, Vernon Hills, IL 60061
Fax: 847-615-0731
E-mail:  sandy@sweepsheet.com
http://www.sweepsheet.com/

Sweepstakes Locator
P.O. Box 686, Morris, IL 60450
E-mail:  sweepslocator@usa.com
http://members.spree.com/family/sweepslocator/

Win A Contest Newsletter
(A newsletter for our Canadian friends)
2-558 Upper Gage St., Suite 108,
Hamilton, ON L8V 4J6
Fax: 905-383-3200
E-mail:  info@winacontest.com
http://www.winacontest.com/

## Internet Web Sites

I love the Internet but really there is so much information
available that sometimes it can just be overwhelming.  It seems
like each contesting site on the Internet links to dozens of others.
I find myself jumping from one to the other to the other until
finally I feel like I'm chasing my tale.

All of the above listed newsletters have web sites with loads of
information for contesters.  Here's a list of twelve more Internet
sites that I like to visit from time to time to see what's new.  All
of these sites provide free information on hundreds of contests
and sweepstakes.  Many of them offer free newsletters by e-mail.

About's Contests and Sweepstakes with Tom Stamatson
http://www.contests.about.com/

Blue House Contest and Sweepstakes Links
http://www.blue-house.com/sweeps/

Cashnet Sweepstakes
http://www.cashnetsweeps.com/

Contests Freebies and Sweepstakes
http://www.contestsfreebiesandsweepstakes.com/

ContestGuide.com
http://www.contestguide.com/

Contest Hound.Com
http://www.contesthound.com/

> There is so much info on the Internet that it can just be overwhelming.

Cooking Contest Central
http://www.recipecontests.com/list.html

Huron On Line
http://www.huronline.com/

Sweepstakes Advantage
http://www.sweepsadvantage.com/

Sweepstakes On Line
http://www.sweepstakesonline.com/

Volition.Com Prize Center
http://www.volition.com/prize.html

Winning Ways
http://www.onlinesweeps.com/

I also like to peek in on Yahoo's sweepstakes and contests message board from time to time. It's fun to hear what people are saying. You can do that at http://groups.yahoo.com/group/SweepsTalk/join.

## Contesting Clubs

Did you know that contesting can be a fun way to meet people? There are Contesting Clubs all over the country. These clubs meet every month on a regular schedule, usually at a restaurant or the food court at a mall. It's always fun to make new friends. They exchange information about contests, swap ideas, inform each other of contests and sweepstakes that are underway and generally congratulate each other on their wins. They also exchange entry blanks, which cuts down on some of the running all over town. Sometimes they enter each other's names and they also trade prizes, in case you win something that you don't need or want you can trade it for something that you can use.

Here's a representative list of Contesting Clubs around the United States, there are many more. If you don't see one in your home town check the phone book or perhaps a club in a nearby state can help you with contact information. If it turns out that there is no Contesting Club in your area, why heck, why not think about starting a club yourself?

Be sure to include a SASE (self addressed stamped envelope) when you write to these clubs. These folks save their own postage stamps for contesting.

Atlantic City Sweepers
151 Dickie Avenue, Staten Island, New York 10314

California Central Cost Sweepers
P. O. Box 1492, Santa Maria, California 93456

Chesapeake Crabs
P. O. Box 153, Damascus, Maryland 20872

Chicago's North & Northwest Suburban Sweeps Club
1636 Churchill Road, Schaumburg, Illinois 60195

Columbus Sweepers
P. O. Box 21125, Columbus, Ohio 43221

Greater Memphis Sweepers
P. O. Box 126, Brunswick, Tennessee 38014

Greater Memphis Sweepers
P. O. Box 163, Arlington, Tennessee 38002

High Cotton Sweepers
501 Elvis Presley Drive, Tupelo, Mississippi 38804

Indiana Rainbows
P. O. Box 24608, Speedway, Indiana 46224

Illiana Sweepers
P. O. Box 775, Hobart, Indiana 46342

Kentuckiana Sweepers
P. O. Box 39512, Louisville, Kentucky 40233

Northern New England Sweepstakes Club
153 Old Hedding Road, #11, Epping, New Hampshire 03042

The Arlington Sweepers
P. O. Box 595243,
Dallas, Texas 75359

> **Contesting Clubs**
> *It's always fun to make new friends!*

The Badger Winners
231 East Park Avenue, Berlin, Wisconsin 54923

The Bay City Sweepers
4 Sissy Lane, Bay City, Texas 77414

The Cactus Clan Sweepers
2209 N. Bull Moose Drive, Chandler, Arizona 85224

The Nebraska Contest Writers and Sweepstakers
412 Avenue C, Plattsmouth, Nebraska 68048

The Dixieland Winners Club
2028 Champions Drive. LaPlace, Louisiana 70068

The Hoosier Winners
11754 Muckshaw Road, Plymouth, Indiana 46563

The Longview Sweepers
2700 Buckner, Longview, Texas 75604

The Northwest Sweepers
1655 South Elm Street, #101, Canby, Oregon 97013

The Queen City Sweepstakers
P. O. Box 3133, Cincinnati, Ohio 45201

The Sin City Sweepers
1606 S. Guilford Dr., Henderson, Nevada 89014

The Winning Team
P. O. Box 634, Pendleton, South Carolina 29670

The Tri-State Sweepstakers
P. O. Box 431, Decorah, Iowa 42101

The Winner's Circle of Southwest Florida
1417 Del Prado, #191, Cape Coral, Florida 33990

# Stop, Look, and Listen

Simply watch for information on contests and sweepstakes as you go through your daily routine. Newsletters, web sites, and clubs are helpful, but there's nothing like just keeping your eyes and ears open. That's how I spot most of the contests that I enter.

To tell you the truth, I don't really like to concentrate too much on widely known contests or those featured in newsletters. You have to compete against all of the other contest enthusiasts. I like to go find my own, preferable in a low volume store. I get excited when I see that kind of sweepstakes.

Look for posters in store windows. One day my husband and I went to Sherwin Williams Paint & Wallpaper shopping for wallpaper. There was the poster right in the window announcing their sweeptstakes. My husband won the car.

Service Merchandiser had a huge banner on the side of their building about a sweepstakes to win matching "His and Hers" watches. I saw the banner, turned my car around, and went to the store to enter the drawing. My daughter Donna and her husband Jim won the watches.

Contests and sweepstakes are often advertised in in-store flyers. Whenever I go to a store I always look through the flyers for entries.

Merchandise displays often advertise contests and sweepstakes. Look for them on the end aisles in grocery and discount stores. You can even find contests and sweepstakes on airplanes. Look for them in the airline magazines. The prize is often a free trip to one of the airline's destination cities. I have picked up thousands of frequent flyer miles while traveling on free trips that I've won! I've taken several trips using these frequent flyer miles. That's like winning another trip!

Bulletin boards in retail stores are another good source for contesting. Watch for new store openings in a chain of stores, these are often promoted with a contest or sweepstakes.

Warranty cards of products purchased may have a sweepstakes entry on it. Quite often there are sweepstakes entries on product coupons. Entries can also be found on a product's box or package.

Your own mailbox can be fertile ground for your hobby. I get a lot of sweepstakes entry forms in the mail, Publisher's Clearing House and Reader's Digest Sweepstakes are two that find there way into almost everyone's mailbox.

## Chapter 6

# Creating the winning entry. Imagination is the key!

---

**In This Chapter**

➤ A day with Oprah
➤ Make your entry standout
➤ Work the chain stores
➤ Always enter family and friends
➤ Successful sweepstakes gimmicks and strategies

---

## Contest vs. Sweepstakes

You might not have stopped to think about how a contest is different from a sweepstakes.  A contest requires you to do something specified in the rules—write an essay, sing a song, or bake a cake, for instance.  A sweepstakes is a <u>drawing</u>, oh you may have to answer a simple question, or send in proof of purchase of the product, but the winner is determined by a random drawing. This chapter is devoted to my strategies for winning sweepstakes. I'm going to tell you the things that you should be doing to become a winner and give you a large number of examples of the success that I am having using these techniques.  I'll get to contest strategies in the next chapter.

## A day with Oprah

I've done some very inventive things with my entry blanks, and that's what it takes to win. One time Channel 5 KSD-TV television in St. Louis was sponsoring a sweepstakes drawing to win a trip to Chicago and a "Day with Oprah". There were entry blanks available at Hardee's restaurants and you could also send in your own postcard entry. I figured that most of the contestants would probably mail in plain U. S. Postal Service postcards so I sent in a picture post card that I happen to have of the Chicago skyline. I hoped the picture postcard would stand out and be noticed.

It worked! My youngest daughter, Diana, went with me and we had a blast! The prize included airfare to Chicago, a limousine ride to the studio, a tour of Harpo studios, and Oprah souvenirs (Oprah mug, Oprah shirt, Oprah hat, etc.). We watched two tapings of the Oprah show, and had a delicious lunch. I was most surprised at the level of security at the Harpo studios, but I found Oprah to be a funny, warm person who is easy to talk to. She even asked me, "How do you win all that stuff? What's your secret?"

My secret is this…

## Make your entry standout

If you are planning to win more than your fair share of sweepstakes you need to put in a little time and effort. Don't worry, it's a fun way to spend your time and really not all that much effort.

I always do something special to my entry blank that makes it different from all of the others. I use colored paper or postcards. I use picture postcards sometimes, as I did in the "Day with Oprah" drawing. Sometimes I draw pictures on my entry blank, or cut out an appropriate picture from a magazine and paste it on the entry blank.

Sometimes I'll fan fold an entry blank to give it a different feel in the entry box. Sometimes I use my pinking shears from my sewing basket to pink the edges of the entry blank. This gives it a different feel.

- **Decorate the entry blank**

- **Fan-fold or laminate the entry blank**

- **Wet the entry blank to stiffen it**

- **Use your pinking shears**

Sometimes I wet an entry blank to make it stiffer when it dries. Sometimes I wet an entry blank with colored water to make it both stiff and distinctive (a double whammy!)

I've even taken my entry blank to Kinko's and had it laminated before I mail it. And while I'm at Kinko's I usually purchase some colorful envelopes and stationary for the next contest or sweepstakes. It might be stationary or envelopes with balloons, animals or flowers on them. These definitely stand out.

Very often I'll try more than one distinguishing gimmick in the same drawing. One time the Upper Deck Baseball Card company was sponsoring a sweepstakes where the prize was to be the "Honorary Manager" of the Cardinals in an "Old-Timer's" baseball game between the 1964 Cardinals and the 1964 Yankees. To try to win the sweepstakes I applied several different gimmicks to my entries. I drew a cardinal bird on one entry with a caption saying, "Cards are #1." I soaked another entry in red food coloring to make the entry stiff and to make it stand out and be noticed. On yet another blank I stuck a sticker of a cardinal bird.

I always send in entries for my friends and family members whenever I enter a sweepstakes and guess what? My son, Donald, won the "Honorary Manager" sweepstakes. Usually the prize awards are not transferable but this time it was and Donald was kind enough to let his father and I go in his place.

**34**

The prize included a celebrity banquet that was held at Lou Brock's restaurant in St. Louis the night before the game. The Master of Ceremonies for the evening was former Cardinal catcher Joe Garagiola. Baseball greats like Lou Brock, Bob Gibson, Curt Flood, Red Schoendienst, and Mickey Mantale were in attendance, as were their wives. There were also a few famous umpires from the '60's.

On the way to the dinner (by the way I had won the evening dress that I wore that night) I stopped and bought five baseballs in hopes of snagging some famous autographs. Many of the players present were members of The Baseball Hall of Fame. The players were very gracious and readily agreed to sign their names on the balls. To this days these autographed balls remain treasured family keepsakes.

The dinner was fantastic! Imagine having dinner with some of the greatest baseball players of all time. These guys were friendly and cordial and acted like you were their next door neighbor. It was a night I'll never forget!

The next day we went to Bush Stadium and watched the game from the Cardinal dugout. Bush Stadium seems really big when you see it from that angle. The players teased their new Honorary Managers with various quips. Bob Gibson said, "Don't work me too hard. I'm an old man you know." Glen Campbell sang the national anthem.

The Cardinals won the World Series in 1964 but the New York Yankees won this game. It was truly a memorable experience. I don't know which of my gimmick entries was picked but I am thankful that one of them was and I was able to be part of the event.

## Work the chain stores

When a chain of stores is having a sweepstakes or contest I try to enter in as many of the area stores as possible. This takes some legwork, but it helps to distribute my entries. If prizes are being given away at each store it's possible to win in more than one store. It's happened to me several times.

_Three TV's At One Time_  After my daughter told me that the Target stores were having a contest to give away a television at each store I drove to a Target to see what kind of a contest the store was sponsoring. It was a participation contest where all I had to do was answer some questions about the new fall line-up on CBS. I brought some entry blanks home with me and found the answers to the questions in the newspaper. I filled out the answers on several of the entry blanks and dropped them in the entry boxes at six different Target stores. It took an afternoon of driving from store to store but it was worth it. I won a television at each of three stores.

_Two 8' toy-filled Christmas socks_  One Christmas the Venture stores had a special sweepstakes at their stores. Each store would be giving away an eight foot long sock filled with toys and games. There wasn't an age restriction in the rules so I could enter all of my grandchildren. My strategy was to go to all of the Venture stores in the area and

> **When a chain of stores is having a sweepstakes or contest I try to enter in as many of the area stores as possible.**

fill out the children's names with bright red and green magic markers. Eight year old Amanda won a sock at one of the stores and five year old Jimmy won a sock at another. The socks were taller than them!

_Two boxes of golf balls_  My son-in-law, Jim, likes to play golf so when K-Mart was sponsoring a golfing trip sweepstakes I tried to win the trip for him. I went to as many different K-Mart stores as I could find and entered his name. I tried some of my proven strategies like fan folding, filling out the blanks with bright magic markers, and crumbling up blanks before dropping them into the entry box. Jim didn't win the trip, but he did win a box of golf balls from two different stores. Hey, a golfer can always use golf balls.

*Four smoke alarms*  To promote "Safety Week" the Venture stores sponsored a sweepstakes with the prize being a smoke alarm to be given away in each store.  I went to several stores in the area and entered all the family's names.  My son-in-law Mark, grandchildren Amanda and Ryan, and I all won a smoke alarm.

*Twenty-eight baseball tickets*  Every summer Shnuck's Grocery Stores sponsor a sweepstakes for St. Louis Cardinal's baseball tickets.  I always drive to several stores and enter all my family so they can have the opportunity to attend a Cardinal game.  I usually draw a Cardinal bird on the entry with various captions such as, "Go Cardinals", or "Cardinals are #1".  So far I've been able to win 28 baseball tickets for my family.

*Nine duffel bags*  I think everybody in my family has a duffel bag.  JC Penny stores sponsored a sweepstakes in the men's department of their stores to give away a duffel bag valued at $100 in each store.  We won a total of nine duffel bags.

*Two giant Bugs Bunny stuffed rabbits*  Bugs Bunny is a character that children just love.  When the Bunny Bread Company sponsored a sweepstake to give away a bugs bunny at the grocery stores where Bunny Bread is sold I decided to try to win a rabbit for my grandchildren and the grandchild of relatives and friends.  I drove to as many of the stores as I could and entered the children's names.  My granddaughter Alynn won one of the rabbit's and my friend Ed's granddaughter Brittny won one as well.  The Bugs Bunny rabbits were huge, taller than the girls.

## Always enter for all your family and friends

Many times the rules of a sweepstakes say that you can only enter once, or that you can only enter once per day.  That's OK.  There's no rule against entering for each member of your family or for each of your friends.  Since I always enter for the whole family occasionally more than one of the bunch will win prizes in an individual sweepstake.

*Four sets of Southwest Airlines tickets (8 tickets)*  Coca-Cola and Southwest Airlines co-sponsored a sweepstakes with the prize being airline tickets to fly anywhere that Southwest flys. They were giving away a total of 24 tickets. My son Donald won two tickets and his wife Debbie won two tickets. They used the tickets to visit Salt Lake City and took Debbie's parents along. My daughter Diana won two tickets, she and her husband went to Lake Tahoe. My friend Ed won two tickets and decided he wanted to visit San Diego. All of these names were selected from one entry box.

*Three awards to do hockey play-by-plays*  My son and two son-in-laws are avid St. Louis Blues hockey fans. Mark even played hockey on a hockey league. When KMOX radio station sponsored a St. Louis Blues "Play-by-Play" sweepstakes I entered all three of the fellows. The rules called for you to send a postcard to the station with name, address, and phone number. I drew a hockey stick on one postcard, a hockey player on another, and musical notes representing the Blues logo on another postcard. Each week a name would be drawn for someone to sit in the announcer's booth at the arena and do a play-by-play of the Blues game. Afterward the winner got to take home a tape as a keepsake of their performance. My son, and two sons-in-law all had their names chosen and announced in consecutive weeks. What a thrill for these hockey fans.

> *Always enter for all of your friends and family!*

*Two wristwatches*  I entered the family in a sweepstakes at Service Merchandise to win wristwatches. I discovered this sweepstake when I saw a big banner hanging on the side of one of the stores. My daughter Donna and her husband Jim each won a beautiful wristwatch.

*Two basketball shoot-outs*  My son Donald and my grandson Jimmy both love to play basketball. My son plays basketball in a firefighter's league and my grandson plays on a team at school. I entered both their names in a sweepstakes I saw in a grocery store. The rules said that I could enter as often as I wished. The prize was the opportunity to compete in a basketball shoot-out at Kiel Auditorium in St. Louis during the half time of the Missouri Valley High School Basketball Tournament. Whoever made the most baskets would win a trip to San Antonio Texas. Both their names were picked along with some other hopefuls. They got to shoot the baskets at Kiel, a thrill for the fellows in itself, but neither of them won the trip.

*Three sporting equipment prizes*   My family loves sports so any time there's a sweepstakes for anything to do with sports I enter their names. A K-Mart close to my house had a drawing for several kinds of sporting equipment. I drew baseballs on some of the entry blanks, crumbled some of the entry blanks, and color dyed some of them. My daughter won a basketball and two of my grandsons each won a baseball and bat set. Jimmy, my 11 year old grandson, is a pitcher on his baseball team so he was delighted when he won a Rawlings batting machine from Nabisco. It was a home run for this family.

*Two 1999 Olympic sweatshirts*   During the 1999 Olympics in Atlanta there were several sweepstakes with Olympic paraphernalia as prizes. I entered some of these sweepstakes and applied some techniques I hoped would work such as decorating entries or envelopes with the Olympic logo, mailing entries in colored envelopes, laminating entries, and even spraying entries with perfume. I don't know which technique worked but my daughter Diana and her husband won Olympic sweatshirts and a professionally framed collection of Olympic pins.

*TV and Nintendo in one drawing*   One day my daughter Donna and I were working a bake sale at a Wal-Mart store to benefit our girl scout troop. We spotted a sweepstakes entry box near the entrance of the store. We filled out some blanks, fan folded them, and dropped them into the box. The next day they called Donna's husband Jim and informed him that he had won a television set. I received a phone call informing me that I had won a Nintendo game.

_Diamond ring and TV drawing_  While shopping at a Grandpa Pigeons store I saw a sweepstakes entry box by the jewelry counter.  I read the rules and learned that several prizes were to be awarded in this sweepstakes.  This is the kind of sweepstakes that I like.  Even though I was in a hurry I took the time to fill out some blanks with my family's names on them.  About a week later they called my son and gave him the good news that he had just won a new 25 inch TV.  He was so excited that he called his sister to tell her.  When she picked up the phone  she was too excited to let him give her the good news because they had just called her and told her that she'd won a diamond ring from the Grandpa Pigeons store.  Both were happy and surprised that the other had won.

## Successful sweepstakes gimmicks and strategies

As you know by now, I've won lots and lots of contests and sweepstakes.  What follows in this chapter is a description of many of the highlights of my contesting career.  They're not in any particular order, I just listed them as they came to mind. I know that I'm tooting my own horn a little bit with this list. Hooray for me!  But that's really not my point at all.  As you read the story of each of these contest wins you should be able to grab a lot of my ideas for yourself.  Remember, I'm not doing anything that you couldn't be doing yourself.  Happy contesting and happy winning!

_Australia and the 2000 Olympics_  Often when I go searching for a sweepstakes I'll walk the perimeter of the store.  Then I walk up and down the aisles to see if there might

> When seaching for a sweepstakes, I search the store looking for an entry box tucked away in some little noticed spot.

be an entry box tucked away in some little noticed spot.  This is how I found the Power Drink sweepstakes.  The prize was a trip to Australia and the 2000 Olympics.

The sweepstakes was an in-store drawing and the entry box was no bigger than a shoe box.  It was on a shelf in an aisle next to the Power Drink product. Power Drink is one of Coca-Cola's products and the sweepstakes was sponsored by the Coca-Cola company.

I looked into the box and saw that there were only a few entries deposited. I took several entries home with me and I filled them out with different family and friend's names printed on each blank. I applied various techniques to the entries hoping that one of the entries would stand out and be chosen.

My daughter Donna's name was chosen and she invited me to accompany her on this once in a lifetime trip. The prize included airfare, hotel accommodations. Coca-Cola being one of the Olympic sponsors had reserved an entire hotel for its staff and friends. Meals were included, as was sightseeing to the Koala Bear Park and a harbor cruise. Tickets to Olympic events each day were included along with transportation to the games.

While we were at the Olympic village we were able to get free food anytime we wanted at the Coca-Cola hospitality building. Donna also received $6,000 spending money. She used part of the money to pay the income taxes on the trip, we used the rest to extend our stay in Australia.

> *Look for out of the way and little noticed entry boxes.*

We saw the Great Barrier Reef. Donna went scuba diving there and was enthralled with what she saw. We visited the Outback, explored the rainforest, and took a boat ride on the Daintree River where crocodiles lay sunning along the shore. Everything that we did on our own was very affordable due to the two-for-one strength of the American dollar versus the Australian dollar.

My grandson Ryan's third grade class at Glendale Elementary School asked us to help them with a special class project—Teddy the Traveling Bear. When they hear that someone is traveling to an exotic destination the class asks if they can send Teddy along. They keep a journal with photographs of all of Teddy's travels.

**41**

Donna and I agreed to take the bear. We were further instructed to pass the bear on to someone from Africa before we returned home and to have that person mail Teddy back to the school after his visit there. Teddy had already been to every continent except for Australia and Africa, so they were hoping to make him a complete global traveler.

Teddy has a backpack which includes a picture of Glendale School and a picture of the class and instructions to be followed for his return.

Donna and I took Teddy everywhere. We photographed him with a kangaroo and a Koala bear, posed in front of the famous Sydney Opera House, and of course at the Olympics.

The Today Show with Katie Coric and Matt Laurer were there covering the events for the folks back home. Matt talked to us about Teddy the Traveling Bear and autographed Teddy's journal. There was a young girl from Africa working at our hotel and she agreed to take Teddy back with her when she returned home. As of this writing Teddy has not returned to Glendale Elementary, but the class is hopeful that he will. He's always come home before.

_**$10,000 Shopping Spree**_  This was the first really big prize that I won. I was looking for a special tote hat for a Christmas gift and I couldn't find it anywhere. I decided to go to an upscale mall in St. Louis called Plaza Frontenac. It's quite a long way from my house, but I thought I might find the item that I'd been looking for there.

While I was in Neiman Marcus I noticed a sweepstakes entry box on a table near a drinking fountain. The entry blanks were sitting there beside the entry box and there was a sign that read, "Win a $10,000 Shopping Spree."

I was in a hurry, but I took the time to fill out an entry which I quickly crumbled and dropped into the box. I was hoping that crumbling the entry would give it more volume and a better chance of being selected.

I was flabbergasted when I heard that I had won. The drawing was conducted at 8:00 AM and my name was announced on the radio. I was still in bed asleep but friends heard my name announced and called to congratulate me. Everyone was so excited, but I was in shock!

A few days later I went back to the mall to claim my prize. They handed me a pretty shopping bag filled with colored tissue and gift certificates totaling $10,000 in denominations of $50 and $100. The good news was that I could share the certificates with my family. I gave each of my nearest and dearest $1,000 which left me with $4,000 to spend on myself.

The sweepstakes sponsors encouraged us to spend the money in as many different stores in the mall as possible. I didn't think that that would be a problem since we could pick from stores like Neiman Marcus, Saks 5th Avenue, and Liz Clayborn, to name a few.

> *I used the $10,000 shopping spree to buy extravagant items that I'd always dreamed of having!*

It was fun going with my family on their mini shopping sprees. When I went shopping for myself I decided to be extravagant and purchase things that I had always dreamed of having but would never actually buy for myself.

The first item I purchased was a $400 Gucci purse. As I was paying for the purse I was overcome with tears of joy. I actually cried! The salesman asked me if there was something wrong with the purse.

The next items I purchased were an $800 leather jacket and a $400 matching skirt. I next picked out some gorgeous Liz Clayborn suits.

I chose some classy dresses at Saks 5th Avenue, with big matching hats. I tried on two sequined evening gowns, one black and one sapphire blue. I couldn't make up my mind which one I wanted so I took them both! Honestly I didn't have a clue where I might where them.

I left the mall with packages galore! Perfume, sweaters, shoes, and even two diamond rings! The timing of this shopping spree couldn't have been better. It was right after Christmas and most of the stores were having big sales. This first big win hooked me on the contesting hobby for sure!

***LHS Chrysler Car*** A sponsor usually reserves the right to substitute a prize of equal or greater value. When we won a sweepstakes sponsored by Sherwin Williams Wallpaper and Paint stores for a new Chrysler Imperial they asked us if we'd accept a Chrysler LHS instead. We said sure! The LHS is the top of the line and it came fully loaded. All we had to decide was what color we wanted.

Everyone dreams of winning a car and what a thrill it can be. We went to a Sherwin Williams Wallpaper and Paint store to buy some wallpaper. As we entered the store I noticed a poster in the window advertising the in-store sweepstakes.

We picked out some wallpaper and then before we left we filled out some entry blanks and dropped them into the entry box. We fan folded the entries to give them more volume so they would be more likely to be drawn.

A few months later we got a call so early in the morning that we were barely awake. When they told us that my husband's name was selected as the Grand Prize winner we thought it was a crank call. They had to convince us that we had actually won. They told us that there were over 400,000 entries in this nationwide sweepstakes.

***Caribbean Cruise*** When the rules of a contest state, "Enter as often as you wish," I will enter the contest everyday, or as often as I can afford the stamps. I sit down and fill out several entries at one time, address the envelopes, and then drop one entry in the mail every day.

To win a Caribbean cruise for my friend Ed I mailed an entry every day for about a month. I applied different techniques to each envelope mailed. I drew a cruise ship on one entry. I used an oversized big purple envelope for another. I wetted some entries in colored water, filled other entries out with bright magic markers, and sprayed perfume on some of the entries. I went to all of this effort in a bid to draw attention to my entry in hopes that it would be chosen. I was determined to win that cruise and I did.

The prize consisted of a 7-day cruise aboard the Carnival cruise ship Destiny. We had a spacious room, with a 25-foot private balcony. We visited the islands of St. Croix, St. Thomas, and the Bahamas. Fabulous!

*San Francisco and San Antonio* One time I glued a picture of the Golden Gate Bridge onto an entry blank to try to win a trip to San Francisco. Almost a year later I received notification that I had won. By that time I'd completely forgotten that I'd even entered. The prize included airfare and hotel accommodations.

While I was on the airplane in route to San Francisco my name was announced on a St. Louis TV station as the winner of a sweepstakes for a trip to San Antonio. There was a requirement though that I had to call the sponsor and claim my prize within a short period of time, otherwise I'd forfeit the prize.

> **To win a Caribbean cruise I drew a cruise ship on one entry, used an oversized purple envelope for another, and wet some entries in colored water.**

My friend Carol Giffhorn saw my name announced on TV, and when she couldn't reach me she called my daughter Donna. Donna called and left an urgent message for me to call home with the desk clerk at the Marriott in San Francisco. Naturally I was a little concerned when I arrived at the hotel and they told me that I needed to immediately call home. Oh my, what bad thing could have happened, I wondered. I did call and my daughter gave me the good news and the telephone number of the TV station where I was to call. I made the call and claimed my prize. You could say that I won a free trip while I was on a free trip.

*Washington D. C.* When my friend Ed won a 7-day trip to San Diego in a sweepstakes sponsored by Shell Oil Company he asked if he could exchange it for a trip to Washington D. C. Shell was nice enough to allow him to do that. Rarely will a sponsor let you substitute one prize for another, it's most unusual.

I spotted this sweepstakes at a Shell station where I buy my gasoline. The cashier behind the counter was singing while I was there and I remarked that he had a good voice. He told me that he'd just made a recording and that I should watch for it in the music stores. I was so impressed with the cashier's voice that I drew musical notes on several entry blanks.

Ed won and we really lucked out. We were in Washington at the peak of cherry blossom time. We got to tour the White House as well as the White House Gardens. The Gardens are only open to tourists twice a year. I bought commemorative White House Easter eggs for my grandchildren, nieces, and Ed's granddaughter Brittny.

*Branson, Missouri* The "Christmas in Branson with the Rockettes" sweepstakes was sponsored by the Shop 'N Save grocery stores. I didn't know if I would have much of a chance to win this sweepstakes because it was being advertised heavily on television.

> *I decorated one postcard with Christmas stickers. I decorated another with red and green bingo dobbers made to look like Christmas ornaments. I dyed some post cards red and some green.*

I wanted to win it though because I'd always heard about the wonderful shows they have in Branson at Christmas time. I also wanted to see the Rockettes again. I saw them one time before at Rockefeller Center in New York City and they were fantastic. I wanted to see them again so I went to the Shop 'N Save store to get an entry.

The entry for this sweepstakes was a postcard provided by Shop 'N Save. According to the rules you could enter as many times as you wished. I tried various techniques. I decorated one postcard with Christmas stickers. I decorated another with red and green bingo dobbers made to look like Christmas ornaments. I dyed some post cards red and some green.

Well some how I won, but what I didn't count on was a blizzard that hit Branson the day we arrived. We couldn't even get out of our hotel. Most of the shows in the area were canceled that night. Fortunately the second day the weather cleared and we were able to see the Rockettes in all their Christmas splendor.

*Denver, Colorado*   I listen to KMOX Radio day and night. One night while I was half asleep I thought I'd heard the announcer say that there was a sweepstakes underway to win a truck. To win you were to send a postcard to the station with your name, address, and phone number.

The next morning I sent in a postcard with one of my drawings on it—a truck. A few weeks later I was notified by mail that I had indeed won the sweepstakes, but the prize wasn't a truck at all. It was a trip to Denver to watch the St. Louis Cardinals play the Colorado Rockies. I guess they liked the drawing of my truck anyway. What a special prize this was for us. We got to watch the game from the announcer's booth with Jack and Joe Buck and Mike Sahnnon. You can't put a price tag on an experience like that! Too bad that the Cardinals lost though.

*St. Petersburg, Florida*   When my daughter Donna won the trip to St. Petersburg, Florida to visit the Cardinal's spring training she and her husband were elated. Both are devoted Cardinal fans so this was a dream come true. The prize included airfare, tickets to Cardinal games, and accommodations at a $400 per night resort. Donna and Jim paid a little extra and brought their two children along.

This contest was sponsored by Car-X Muffler and Brake shops and KMOX Radio. You could enter as many times as you wished and the winner's name would be announced on KMOX.

I visited several Car-X shops in the area and dropped off entry blanks filled out on behalf of my family and friends. I had colored the entries bright yellow, Car-X's corporate color. I had also address some yellow index cards since this was a permitted entry blank. Donna was the lucky winner!

*Dinner with Marshal Faulk*   This sweepstakes was sponsored by the Tostitos Pizza Company. I saw the entry blanks next to the entry box by the frozen pizza display case at Schnuck's grocery store. I took some of the entries home with me. I wetted them in water to make the blanks stiff. Some paper gets stiff after it gets wet and the stiffer blanks are more likely to be chosen in a drawing. I returned the stiffened filled out blanks to the store and dropped them in the box.

About two weeks before the Rams big Super Bowl game against the Tennessee Titans I got the call informing me that I had won. The prize was a dinner with Rams football players Marshal Faulk and Trent Green at Ozzie Smith's restaurant in St. Louis. Ozzie Smith is a retired Cardinal short stop. Ozzie Smith was there with the two football players. Before dinner I played a football video game with Mr. Faulk on a big screen TV. He sacked my quarterback twice but I didn't care. It was all fun and I got autographed footballs for my grandsons.

*River Cruise with Radio Personality*   KMOX Radio sponsored a sweepstakes to win a Mississippi River cruise on the Becky Thatcher riverboat with radio personality Jim White and his wife Pat. I am a big fan of "The Bumper" as White is known so I wanted to win the cruise.

The rules called for postcards to be mailed to the station with name, address, and phone. My strategy for this sweepstakes was that I drew a boat on my postcard with the name "Patty Wagon" printed on the side of the boat, which is what Jim White calls his own boat.

I won and the cruise was great! There was a delicious dinner and a jazzy ragtime band for entertainment. An added plus for me was that Captain Bill Carroll was on board. Captain Carroll was my boss when I worked on the S. S. Admiral while I was in high school. The Admiral was a famous St. Louis excursion boat that cruised the Mississippi for many years. It's now permanently moored at the St. Louis riverfront and used as a casino.

_**Breakfast with Muni Opera Stars**_ "The Muni" is a famous outdoor theater in St. Louis that is very dear to my heart. The old place holds a lot of memories for me. When I heard that KMOX Radio was having a drawing for breakfast at the Muni with the stars appearing in the current production I decided to try to win.

Some of the stars that would be at the breakfast were Van Johnson, John Davidson, Carol Lawrence, John James, Marge Champion and Art Fleming. My strategy to win this sweepstakes was to draw red socks on my postcard. Red socks are a Van Johnson trademark.

My entry was chosen and I got to have breakfast at the outdoor rehearsal studio where the performers rehearse for the Muni shows. This was especially exciting for me because I'd danced at the Muni as a child and had rehearsed at this very studio. The breakfast was delicious and the stars delightful. A special surprise guest at the breakfast was former St. Louis Cardinal great Lou Brock. He was wearing his impressive 1964 World Series ring.

_**Tickets to "My Fair Lady"**_ This past summer, "My Fair Lady" was performed at The Muny. The St. Louis Post Dispatch newspaper invited readers to design a hat that Eliza Doolittle of "My Fair Lady" might wear to the Ascot Races. My eight year old granddaughter Hannah was keen to enter. There were three categories in the contest; adult, student, and child.

Hannah won the child's category with her romantic yellow and read boater hat. The strategy she implemented was to glue big silk flowers on her drawing to give her hat a 3-D effect.

For her efforts Hannah won four tickets to the "My Fair Lady" production. She also received a plague and she was one of the guests of honor at a special tea where her hat was displayed.

_**Speaking role in radio show**_  I was intrigued when I heard the announcement on KMOX Radio that they were running a sweepstakes involving their annual holiday Christmas show that they do every year for charity.  The prize was that the winner and a friend would get to be part of the show, speaking parts no less.

I thought it would be a challenge to win the part and to perform the role on the air.  The real reason I wanted to win however was so I could meet all of the radio personalities and be able to put a face to all of the folks that I listened to so regularly.

The rules called for you to mail a postcard to the station with name, address, and phone.  To enhance my chances of winning I decorated a postcard with a Santa Claus sticker.  I drew a radio microphone in front of Santa with musical notes coming from Santa's mouth, as if he was singing on the radio.  My postcard must have drawn the attention of the judges because I got a call soon after mailing it to let me know that I had won.

I was informed that there was to be a rehearsal the night before the show.  My friend Carol Giffhorn agreed to do the other role in the play.  She's also a big fan of KMOX.  At the rehearsal Carol and I got to meet all the radio personalities who were in the show.  Practically everyone who works at KMOX participates.  We also got to meet some of the sponsors of the show.

My part called for me to scream because radio personality Jim White had stolen my cheese sandwich.  I had no idea how sensitive radio microphones are and I screamed as loud as I could to ensure that I would be heard.  The radio engineer fell off of his stool exclaiming that I had blown the earwax right out of his ears! Embarrassed, I asked if I should scream a little softer for the broadcast the next night.  He said, "Oh no.  Scream the same way.  I'll just be better prepared for it the next time."

The next day KMOX ran promotional commercials all day long plugging that evening's Christmas show.  The promo's said, "Tune in to the KMOX radio holiday show tonight and hear Carol Shaffer scream!"  Well, I took a lot of good natured teasing,

**50**

but I knew that it was all in fun. The show went over great to a sellout audience at the Westport Theater and to listeners throughout the Midwest.

*Grocery cart race*   When I saw a sweepstakes underway at Dierberg Grocery with a grocery cart race at a St. Louis Rams game as the prize I thought this was the perfect contest for my family. Most of my family love football, especially the Rams. The prize also included four tickets to the game the day of the cart race.

I tried to think of some unusual gimmicks that might get a member of my family choosen. The sweepstakes was an in-store drop-in-the-box drawing. The entry blanks were not very big, but I managed to draw a football on a few blanks. I color dyed some blanks in the Ram's colors, blue on one end and yellow/gold on the other end. I fan folded some of the blanks and put football stickers on others.

> **I drew a football on a few blanks, color dyed some blanks in the Ram's colors, fan folded some of them, and put football stickers on others.**

I don't know which gimmick worked but my friend Ed's name was drawn. Ed had a scheduling conflict so my son-in-law Mark took his place. He was to go out on the field right before the game pushing his grocery cart. Three parachutes were to be dropped from the ceiling of the dome. If Mark caught one parachute he would win a $100 Dierberg gift certificate. If he caught two parachutes he'd win $300, and if he caught all three he'd win a $500 Dierberg gift certificate.

Mark caught two parachutes, but only received one $100 gift certificate. According to the rules the whole parachute had to land inside the cart and one of Mark's catches was draped over the side of the cart. He missed the third parachute entirely.

Pushing a grocery cart on a football field is more difficult than it appears. It feels like you are pushing a cart through thick grass, the artificial turf is that thick. I know because the following year

I entered the whole family in the same sweepstakes again. This time my daughter Diana won. She couldn't participate because she had to work so I took her place. I could hardly push the cart! It was a sellout crowd and thousands of people cheered me on but I only managed to catch one of the parachutes. What an experience!

_Lionel Train Set_  My son-in-law Mark loves trains. He subscribes to train magazines, studies old train schedules, and collects miniature trains so he was thrilled when I won a Lionel train set for him. He would have been even more excited if he had won the Grand Prize—a trip on an old steam engine. My strategy for this sweepstakes was to apply a train sticker to the entry and draw a train on the envelope, complete with smoke swirling from the smokestack.

_Nintendo Game_  One Christmas my Daughter Diana called to tell me that the Target stores were sponsoring an in-store, drop-in-the-box sweepstakes in the electronics department. The prize was a Nintendo game with one to be given away in each store. My grandson Ryan wanted a Nintendo for Christman so I offered to try to win it for him.

The deadline for entering was getting pretty close. I went to the nearest store and got a few entry blanks. I brought them home and wet them in water so they would dry stiff. I filled them out and returned them to the store the next day. Ryan got a new Nintendo for Christmas.

_Day at a Spa_  Most women dream about enjoying a day at a luxurious spa. My daughter Donna found just how much fun it is after I entered her name in a "Day at a Spa" sweepstakes.

All of the sweepstakes entry blanks were gone when I went to the store to enter the family's names, but the information on the entry box explained that you could also enter using three by five inch index cards. I mailed colored index cards bearing pretty flowery stickers. I even stuck some "smiley-face" stickers from Wal-Mart on a few of them. Donna's name was chosen and she enjoyed a day she will long remember.

_Diamond Solitaire Pendant Necklace_    The sponsor of the "Christmas Wish List" sweepstakes was National Food Stores, and the Grand Prize was a big screen television.  What I liked about this contest was that there were several other prizes that would be awarded.  I tried a new technique for this sweepstakes that I had never tried before.  I went to Kinkos and had the entry blank laminated to make it stand out and be noticed.  A few days later they notified me that I'd won fifth place; a diamond solitaire pendant necklace.  The necklace is

> **I tried a new technique for this sweepstakes that I had never tried before. I went to Kinkos and had the entry blank laminated to make it stand out.**

beautiful and I probably enjoy it more than I would have the big screen TV.  Another surprise with this sweepstakes is that the sponsor paid the taxes on the prize.  That hardly ever happens!

_Sears Gift Certificate_    During the Christmas holidays a Sears store close to my home sponsored a "Wheel of Fortune" sweepstakes.  The prize was a $500 gift certificate.  I drew a colorful "Wheel of Fortune" design on both sides of the white entry blank.  I drew pictures on both sides of the entry blank so that my artwork would be visible no matter which way the entry fell into the box.  I also printed "Sears" in the middle of each wheel.  I was notified soon after that I'd won!  My first thought was that I could use the gift certificate to buy Christmas presents, and I did just that!

_Concert Tickets_    Concerts appeal to people of all ages, young and old alike, so anytime I see a concert sweepstakes I will enter the entire family.  We have won a total of 16 concert tickets.  My strategy for concert tickets is that I apply some sort of musical gimmick to my entry, such as drawing musical notes or using stickers with a musical theme.  For one sweepstakes I spray painted the entry on one side with gold paint, and while the paint was still wet I sprinkled it with gold glitter to give the blank a theatrical look.

**53**

_Air Hockey Table_  It isn't everyday that a big air hockey table valued at $2,000 is delivered to your house but that's what happened after I entered my family's names in the "Get-Away Ski" sweepstakes.  I found the in-store sweepstakes at a Schnuck's store.  The Grand Prize was a ski trip to Colorado.  We didn't win that but my son-in-law Mark did win the hockey table as First Prize.  My strategy for this sweepstakes was to color the border of the entry with bright colored magic markers on both sides.  Whatever way the entry blank landed in the entry box the bright colors could be seen.

_Red Bird Roost Party_  Talk about fun!  When my friend Ed won a party for 10 people in Coca-Cola's "Red Bird Roost" at Bush Stadium we all had a great time.  Imagine being able to watch a Cardinal baseball game while seated on plush, soft, leather couches, drinking all the Coca-Cola you want, and eating pizza to your heart's content.  I used various techniques on this one, such as drawing a Cardinal bird on an entry and writing "I love Coke!" on another.

JACKPOT! Carol Shaffer with her new car and other winnings. She's also won a shopping spree, a cruise and a trip to Hawaii — and she doesn't count on luck!

My contesting has brought me a lot of publicity. Here's my picture as it appeared in the *National Enquirer.*

This is a picture that appeared in my hometown newspaper, the *Monroe County Clarion Journal.* That's me with Debbye Turner, Miss America 1990.

Former Miss America Debbye Turner sent me this nice note after taping a segment for the "Show Me St. Louis" TV show.

**5** KSDK TV • 1000 Market Street • Saint Louis • Missouri 63101

2-15-99

Carol—

It was pleasure meeting you and Don. Congratulations on all of your success. I do hope you like the story we aired about you on Show Me St. Louis.

Here are your photos. Thanks so much for dropping them off at the station. I'm also returning the newspaper article about you, just in case you need it.

Keep winning!

Debbye Turner

Show Me St. Louis

How do you like the hat? This picture appeared in *The Examiner*. Sometimes you just can't be too flamboyant in contesting. It always pays to try to attract extra attention to yourself.

Clipping from the
*Monroe County
Clarion Journal*

# Santa brings area woman $10,000 shopping spree

### By MARVIN CORTNER
### Staff Writer

Caroleen Ruth Shaffer of Columbia received an unexpected gift from Santa Claus this year—a $10,000 shopping spree at Plaza Frontenac in St. Louis.

The shopping spree giveaway was a promotion sponsored by merchants in the Plaza Frontenac mall and by KMOX Radio. Shaffer's name was drawn for the spree on Dec. 20.

"I go to Plaza Frontenac once and a while because my daughter lives out that way," said Shaffer on Thursday, a week after winning the prize. While shopping at the mall, Shaffer, and about 50,000 other shoppers, filled out name and address cards and dropped them into boxes in the different stores. The boxes were then later dumped together and mall and radio officials drew the winning name.

Caroleen Shaffer

"I'll be receiving the $10,000 in $50 and $100 gift certificates that can be used in any of the stores," Shaffer said. "I have to use them before May 15."

But Shaffer, despite winning the big spree, was a little disappointed.

"My plan at first was to use the $10,000 at a travel agency in the mall and go to Europe," Shaffer said. "But I couldn't do that. I have to use it for merchandise."

Shaffer said she's going to share her good fortune with her three children, her mother, her sister and her husband, Donald. For herself, she's been compiling a dream list.

"I want to get some nice designer cloths and some jewelry and a new watch for myself," Shaffer said. "I also want to buy a complete outfit for my husband—including a suit, top coat, hat and new watch.

"I wanted some things for the house and a new computer but there aren't any stores there that carry what I want. They have mostly clothing and jewelry.

"When I do go shopping, it's going to be a lot of fun—I want to buy some winter things now and wait until later to buy summer clothes."

See SPREE, page 2A

Clarion Journal (*) • Wednesday, January 19, 2000 • Page A3

**WS**

# Resident plays ball with Rams

## She had dinner with Faulk, Green

**By Garen Vartanian
Staff writer**

Columbia resident Caroleen Shaffer spent December becoming well acquainted with the St. Louis Rams.

Thanks to winning a contest sponsored by Totino's Pizza, Shaffer had dinner with Rams running back Marshall Faulk and quarterback Trent Green at Ozzie Smith's restaurant last month.

After dinner, Shaffer played John Madden 2000, a football game for the Sega-Genesis system, against Faulk. Shaffer, however, did not fare so well.

**COLUMBIA**

"He cremated me," Shaffer said. "I only gained a couple of yards. But it was all in fun. Marshal was really nice. So was Trent Green."

Shortly thereafter, Shaffer won a contest sponsored by Dierberg's Grocery Store. Shaffer's reward was a visit to the Trans World Dome where she participated in another contest on the field prior to St. Louis' game against the Chicago Bears Dec. 26.

Three parachutes were dropped on the field. If Shaffer caught one in her grocery cart, she received a $100 gift certificate to Dierberg's. If Shaffer caught two parachutes, she earned a $300 gift certificate.

Had she corralled all three, Shaffer would have won a $500 gift certificate. As it stood, Shaffer nabbed one parachute.

Later, Shaffer met Rams players and head coach Dick Vermeil as the team took the

Submitted photo

Columbia resident Caroleen Shaffer enjoys a fun moment with St. Louis Rams quarterback Trent Green. Shaffer had dinner with Green and Rams running back Marshall Faulk at Ozzie Smith's restaurant in the middle of December.

field. Shaffer also received free tickets to the game and watched St. Louis defeat Chicago.

Shaffer is a prolific contest winner, earning better than $100,000 in prizes the past five years.

Shaffer, who will appear in the April issue of Good Housekeeping because of her success in contests, even has her own Win Big Video.

Anyone interested in the video may call (800) 341-1607. Shaffer also has a web page, which is www.winbigprizes.com.

Here I am pictured with former Saint Louis Rams quarterback Trent Green. He and I had a dinner date!

**59**

This is the nice letter that they sent to us when we won the Chrysler automobile.

Advertising Production Sèrvices Corporation

May 5, 1993

*Rec'd 7 MAY 93*

Mr. Don Shaffer
303 W. Legion
Columbia, Illinois 62236

Dear Mr. Shaffer:

CONGRATULATIONS! You are the Grand Prize Winner in the "Sherwin Williams and Imperial Drive Home the Savings Sweepstakes 3!"

Your entry form was picked from thousands of entries and entitles you to claim the following prize:

    * A 1993 Chrysler Imperial

Enclosed is an Affidavit of Eligibility, Release and Prize Acceptance form to have you complete, have notarized and send back in the enclosed envelope by May 21, 1993. If the enclosed form is not completed and received at our offices by that time, your prize will be forfeited.

Upon receiving the completed Affidavit, we will coordinate the delivery of the 1993 Chrysler Imperial.

Congratulations Again!

Sincerely,

ADPRO

Jeff Resnick
Manager, Account Services

JR:pj

Enclosure

*JEFF CALLED AND SAID CHRYSLER (DETROIT) DID NOT HAVE ANY '93 MODELS AVAILABLE. HE ASKED "WOULD YOU ACCEPT A '94 CHRYSLER LHS"? I REPLIED YES!*

4400 Emery Industrial Parkway, Cleveland, Ohio 44128   (216) 464-2055   FAX (216) 464-3884

To our delight, they awarded us a '94 Chrysler LHS instead of the '93 Imperial that had been the advertised prize.

Here I am with some of the other contestants in the Ms. Senior Illinois pageant. I enjoy meeting new challenges, and this contest was something new for me.

# MidwestLiving

1912 Grand Avenue • Des Moines, IA 50309-3379 • 515-284-3721   Fax 515/284-3836

June 6, 1995

Caroleen Shaffer
303 West Legion
Columbia, IL  62236

Dear Caroleen,

Congratulations!  You are the grand prize winner in the *Midwest Living* magazine Aisles of Discovery Sweepstakes Contest.  Your name was selected from entries submitted to Schnucks Markets, Inc.  You have won an exciting trip for four to the Hawaiian Island of your choice.

Simply select your dates (must be used by May 1, 1996), and subject to availability.  MLT Northwest Vacations will provide air transportation from major Midwest gateway locations to the Hawaiian island destination of your choice.  Budget will provide one rental car on the island of your choice for the 5-7 days that you select.  Aston Hotels & Resorts will provide hotel accommodations on the island of your choice for your group (2 double rooms) for 5-7 nights during your selected time.  Also included in your prize are golf tee-times for two and a set of FX clubs by Ram Golf provided by Healthy Choice.

In order to be eligible to receive your grand prize you must complete the enclosed Release, Travel Companion Liability Release, and Affidavit of Eligibility forms within 10 days of notification of your prize.  Each person traveling with you, including minors, must also complete the appropriate forms to be eligible to travel.

Again, congratulations on being the grand prize winner in the *Midwest Living* Aisles of Discovery Sweepstakes Contest.  Please contact me for further details at 515/284-3422.

Sincerely,

*Barbara J. Rasko*

Barbara J. Rasko
Special Events Manager

**M**eredith
CORPORATION

**62**

My friend Martha Berry and I are pictured here on a trip to Hawaii. No trip to Hawaii would be complete without a traditional Hawaiian Luau.

05/06/98

RUTH SHAFFER
303 W LEGION
COLUMBIA, IL  62236

Dear  RUTH,

**Congratulations!  You have been selected as one of the lucky first prize winners in the Sears _Wheel of Fortune/Jeopardy!_ "Play To Win" promotion.  As a first prize winner, you have won Sears gift certificates valued at $500.**

Enclosed, please find your prize - Five (5) $100 Sears Gift Certificates*.  Use these gift certificates just like cash to purchase merchandise at any Sears.

*Redeemable for merchandise and services at any Sears store in the United States.  Not redeemable for cash.  Accepted as payment on Sears Card Accounts._

We are pleased to be able to offer exciting promotions to all our valued Sears customers.  We hope you enjoy these gift certificates during your next visit to Sears.

Thank you for participating in the Sears **"Play To Win"** promotion.  If you are interested in learning about future Sears promotions,  keep looking in-store for details or visit our web site at www.Sears.com.

Best Regards,

Audra Hicks
Sales Promotion Specialist

ref5901

I drew a colorful "Wheel of Fortune" design on both sides of the white entry blank for this contest.  I also printed "Sears" in the middle of each wheel.  As you can see, it worked!

KSDK • • • • 1000 Market Street • • • • St. Louis, Missouri 63101 • • • • 314/421-5055

May 18, 1994

*Rec'd may 19*

Caroleen Shaffer
303 W. Legion
Columbia, IL 62236

Dear Caroleen:

Congratulations! You have been selected as a winner in the
"Watch and Win with Oprah Contest" on Channel Five.
This is a letter to verify that you are indeed a winner.

As a winner, you and a guest will enjoy a trip to Chicago to
see a live taping of the Oprah Winfrey Show, lunch at the
Drake Hotel in Chicago and round trip transportation on
Southwest Airlines. You will need to provide your own
transportation to and from the airport in St. Louis on the date
of your trip.

You will be contacted next fall to give you further details
of your prize. Again, congratulations on being a winner,
and keep watching Oprah on Channel Five!

Sincerely,

*Scott Hill*

Scott Hill
Contest Coordinator

MULTIMEDIA, INC.

**65**

My trip to Chicago to see a taping of the Oprah show is a day
that I will never forget. Here's a picture of my daughter Diana
and I with Oprah herself! Oprah is as gracious in person
as she appears to be on TV.

That's me with John O'Hurley host of "To Tell the Truth".
I've met lots of celebrities through my contesting.

# BBDO
## HOUSTON

SEPTEMBER 20, 2000

EDWARD REINBOLD
2827 B LEMAY FERRY
ST. LOUIS, MO 63125

Dear Mr. Reinbold:

CONGRATULATIONS! Your name has been drawn as an apparent Shell/St. Louis Cardinals Scorecard Sweepstakes winner of a trip for two to San Diego on September 25, 2000 through October 2, 2000, valued at approximately $2,820. In order to receive your prize, you must comply with the requirements as stated in the Official Rules and the directions below.

Please complete and return the enclosed Affidavit of Eligibility and Liability/Publicity ("Affidavit") Release. By signing this Affidavit, you certify that you have read and met all of the Official Rules and are fully eligible to win a prize. This Affidavit also releases the Sponsors from any liability that maybe caused by the prize. A copy of the Official Rules is enclosed for your reference.

Also enclosed is an Affidavit of Release of Liability that must be completed and signed by your guest. This Affidavit releases the Sponsors from any liability that may be caused by the prize.

These Affidavits are legally binding documents that will effect your rights and those of your guest. Before signing, you and your guest should read them carefully and make sure that you both understand all of the terms. If you are a minor, the prize must be awarded in the name of your parent or legal guardian and the parent or legal guardian must complete and submit the Parent/Legal Guardian section of the Affidavit. A minor must be accompanied by a parent or legal guardian on the trip.

Both Affidavits must be completed and signed by you and your guest before a Notary Public and returned to us via fax at (713) 585-6555 no later than 12:00pm on 9/21/00. Please send the original notarized, signed documents to Dee Kilkenny BBDO Houston 1800 West Loop South, Suite 600, Houston, TX 77027 via Federal Express Priority Overnight Service (please use account number 2187-0567-7 so that you will not incur shipping charges) for arrival on Friday, September 22, 2000. If we do not receive the faxed documents by 12:00 p.m. on 9/21/00, followed up by the original completed Affidavits by 12:00pm on 9/22/00, you will automatically forfeit your prize. If you have any questions, please call me.

Notice the request for affidavits that must be signed before a notary public. There are a lot of legal angles to contesting. You really have to watch your P's and Q's.

**KMOX**

CBS Radio
A Division of CBS Inc.
One Memorial Drive
St. Louis, Missouri 63102-2498
(314) 621-2345

July 20, 1994

Mrs. Caroleen Shaffer
303 W. Legion
Columbia, IL  62236

Dear Mrs. Shaffer:

I hope that your trip to Denver was very enjoyable!  Too bad the Cardinals didn't cooperate and give you some wins, though.

As promised, I wanted to let you know the total value of the trip.  I finally heard back from all of the vendors, and the total value is $1,157.00. Enclosed are copies of the signed affidavits stating the values of the individual prizes, and copies of the baseball tickets which show the value.

Early in 1995 you will receive a 1099 Misc. Income Tax Form from KMOX/CBS Inc. in the amount of $1,157.00.  You are required to file this form with your 1994 income taxes.

If you have any questions, don't hesitate to call me. (314-444-3289).

Sincerely,

Jacki Huffman
Promotion Coordinator

69

## CONGRATULATIONS!

MLT Vacations is pleased to present you with a trip for two to Las Vegas, Nevada!
You'll enjoy MLT's famous worry-free service to one of the hottest travel
destinations around.

Your worry free vacation includes:
• Roundtrip air transportation for two to Las Vegas from St.Louis for four nights.
• Roundtrip airport/hotel transfers.

Terms and Conditions:
• The airfare rules stated in the Las Vegas brochure apply (copy enclosed).
• Tickets have no cash value and can only be used by the recipient.
• Trip is valid for travel to Las Vegas only. No substitutions will be allowed.
• Travel must be booked by February 29, 2000.
• Travel must be completed by May 31, 2000.
• Space is subject to program dates and availability.
• Additional charges for taxes, misc. fees and surcharge dates are the
  responsibility of the recipient.

The enclosed certificate works just like a gift certificate.  Just provide it to MLT
Vacations as your payment.
To help with booking, please be prepared to provide your assigned trip winner number,
located in the upper right corner of your certificate.

*Give me Call- and I discuss all
the details with you!*

*Leslie Johnson*

# Congratulations!

On behalf of Silver Dollar City, Inc., KMOV, Shop 'N Save and Coca-Cola I would like to extend my congratulations on winning the Branson Grand Holiday Sweepstakes! This prize package includes the following:

- 4 tickets to see the World's Biggest Christmas Show, the Radio City Christmas Spectacular, starring the world-famous Rockettes
- 4 one-day tickets to Silver Dollar City's Old Time Christmas Festival
- 4 tickets aboard the Showboat Branson Belle
- 2 nights hotel accommodations at Howard Johnson Hotel in Branson

Enclosed in this package you will find everything that you will need in order to enjoy a holiday family getaway to Branson! Please keep in mind that many of the contents of this prize package expire December 16, 2000, so make your plans now!

1) To reserve your hotel room, call the Branson location for Howard Johnson at (417)336-5151 or 888-336-3212 and ask for the general manager, Howard Kitchen. Check the brochure for directions to this property located just off of Hwy 76. Present the certificate upon arrival at the hotel. To insure availability, I recommend that you make this reservation first.
2) To redeem your tickets for the Radio City Christmas Spectacular, starring the Rockettes, please call the Silver Dollar City reservation center at 1-800-5-PALACE and reference the certificate in this package with the promotional title and numbers found in the lower right hand corner of the voucher. For best seating, please make these reservations as soon as possible!
3) Silver Dollar City tickets may be redeemed at the front gate entrance upon arrival. Please check brochures for dates and hours of operation. Silver Dollar City is closed Mondays and Tuesdays for the months of November and December. You may call the Silver Dollar City reservation center at 1-800-952-6626 with any questions.
4) To make reservations aboard the Showboat Branson Belle call 1-800-952-6626 and reference the small tan card found in this package. This is redeemable for four people aboard the "Cirque Fantastique" lunch cruise or the "Steppin' Out" early dinner cruise. This does not include gratuity, souvenir drinks or photos. Check the brochure for times and schedule of cruises. Present card when picking up your tickets.

Again, congratulations on winning and we look forward to your stay in Branson!

Sincerely,

*J. Scholten*

Tammy Scholten
Promotions Manager

HCR 1 Box 791 • Branson, Missouri 65616-9602 • 417/338-2611

I'd always wanted to see the world-famous Radio City Rockettes
This contest gave me my chance!

I consider my trip to Australia to see the Olympics one of the highlights of my life. It was a once in a lifetime experience. This was my official ID card as a guest of Coca-cola.

Here's my daughter Donna and I and Teddy the Traveling Bear
outside Sydney's famous Opera House.

I made a lot of friends in Australia. This furry fellow is a
little guy that I particularly enjoyed meeting.

March 16, 2000

To:      Carol Shaffer

From:   Amy Stone

# CONGRATS!

You have won a 32" Color TV!

Enclosed is a form for you to fill out and return to me
(envelope included!) and I will mail back a copy to you.  And
I have included my business card in case you have any
questions!

Enjoy and thanks for entering the HGTV Dream Home
Giveaway 2000!

*3660 SOUTH GEYER ROAD ❀ SUITE 250 ❀ SAINT LOUIS, MO 63127-1223 ❀ 314-984-8900 ❀ FAX 314-984-8884*

As you can see, I enjoy collecting these "You Have Won" letters.
I'm only sharing a few of them in this book.  If I included them
all that would be a book in itself!

# STELLA FOODS, INC.

STELLA • FRIGO • GARDENIA • TOLIBIA • INTERNATIONAL

*Rec'd Nov. 16*

November 14, 1994

Ms. Caroleen Shaffer
303 W. Legion
Columbia, IL  62236

Dear Ms. Shaffer,

You are one of the **first place prize winners** for the Lorraine Cheese "Picnic in Paris" Sandwich Contest.  In appreciation for your outstanding efforts you have won a West Bend Automatic Bread Maker complete with an instructional video. The bread maker will arrive within four weeks.

Thank you for entering the Lorraine Cheese "Picnic in Paris" Sandwich Contest and once again... Congratulations!

Sincerely,

Stella Foods

P.O. Box 19024  •  Green Bay, WI 54307-9024  •  414/494-2228  •  Fax 414/494-7717

I think I get as big a kick out of winning the smaller prizes as I do when I win a prize that's really big.  My family and I have really enjoyed this bread maker that I won in a Lorraine Cheese contest.

Here's my friend Ed and I as we are about to depart on a fabulous Caribbean cruise on the Carnival ship Destiny. We mailed an entry for this contest every day for a month!

All ashore that's going ashore!

My friend Ed says I'd make a good "pin-up girl",
but I don't know about that.

I glued a picture of the Golden Gate Bridge onto my
entry blank to win my trip to San Francisco.

While I was on my trip to San Francisco I learned that
I'd won a trip to San Antonio!  Here's me in front of the Alamo.

My son, Donald, and daughter, Diana, in the Schnucks
"Dome Drop" held just before a St. Louis Rams game.
They each won a $300 Schnucks gift certificate!

*What's Up Doc?*
I've won prizes for all my grandchildren.
It's one of the best bonus of contesting!
This is my granddaughter, Alynn.

## Chapter 7

# Participation Contests Showcase Your Talent!

Participation contests are challenging. They test your skill, expertise, and creativity. I like participation contests because it gives me a chance to show-off my abilities in a context that's often quite far afield from my daily routine.

## Essay contests

I like to write so naturally I like essay type contests. One of the best things about essay contests is that there usually aren't as many entries. Many people think it's too much work to write an essay, or they think that they probably aren't clever enough to come up with the winning piece. That's fine with me if that's the way they feel. It just means there are fewer contesters out there competing with me for the grand prize.

You don 't see as many essay contest advertised because sponsors don't offer them as often as sweepstakes. There are two reasons for that. Number one, a contest or sweepstakes is usually conceived as a promotion for whatever it is that the sponsor is selling. Consequently they want their contest to generate as much interest as they can, from as many people as they can. The other reasons that there are fewer essay contests is that they require the sponsor to do more work. All of the entries have to be individually read and judged. That's a lot more trouble than simply pulling a name out of a hat.

Still, there are enough essay contests underway at any one time that a person could, if he or she wanted to, establish essay and word type contests as their specialty and forget about entering sweepstakes all together. Hey, contesting is just a hobby. There is no right or wrong way to do it. Like Burger King says, you might as well "Have It Your Way." (I wonder if that slogan by any chance came from a contest.)

> **There are enough essay contests underway at any one time that a person could establish essay and word type contests as their specialty.**

In a five-minute look-see on the Internet I came up with essay contests underway on a variety of topics. One contest asked for an essay on a spiritual or supernatural theme, another called for a humorous essay, another contest required a love story, and yet another contest asked for a country music song. You name the subject and there's probably an essay contest involving it. Have fun!

Here's a few examples of some essay contests that I've won over the years.

_**Opportunity to Do a TV Commercial**_  One day while I was watching my favorite soap opera, The Young and The Restless on KMOV TV I heard them announce an essay type contest sponsored by the TV station. The prize was the opportunity to do a commercial for that particular soap opera.

**82**

I love these kind of prizes. They don't have any monetary value yet to me they are priceless. I call these fun, or adventure prizes, like my Day with Oprah, the Dinner with Marshal Faulk, or the chance for a role in the KMOX Radio Christmas show. When I heard about this contest to be in a TV commercial I jumped for my pencil to write down the rules and entry information.

Contestants were to write an essay about their favorite character on *The Young and The Restless*, in 100 words or less. My strategy for this one was to try to take a little bit different approach then what I thought most people would take. I assumed that most of the contestants would write about the good guys, the stars of the show. To make my entry different and catch the attention of the judges I decided to write about Jill Abbott, the trouble maker on the show. It wasn't easy to come up with many endearing qualities about Jill but apparently I managed. I won the contest!

> *Even though lacking monetary value, I still love the kind of prizes that give me the chance for a fun adventure!*

I went to the station and did the commercial, which mostly consisted of reading what I had written. Afterward they gave me a tour of the TV station. I met several TV personalities and observed how things work from the news room to the weather room.

I might mention that the weather department at KMOV-TV sponsors a sweepstakes called "Count on Kent". Viewers send postcards to the station for a drawing to win two umbrellas, one adult and one child. The umbrellas have the station's logo on them. I've won this sweepstakes twice. My strategy is to draw a colorful umbrella on my postcard, with rain coming down. I also printed KMOV-4 on the umbrellas.

*Trip For Two to Las Vegas*  When MLT, a travel agency, sponsored an essay contest about "Mothers" I jumped at the chance to win. The prize was a trip for two to Las Vegas.

The contest required an essay describing why your mother deserves a trip, in 100 words or less. I wrote about how much my mother loves to travel, and to what lengths she will go to finance her passion for it. She bakes and sells decorated cookies, she makes and sells crafts. She even took a part-time job one time taking the muscle measurements of football players!

The judges must have been impressed by my mother's efforts because my essay was chosen as the winning entry!

*Speech for a Senator* Illinois Senator Ralph Dunn sponsored an unusual essay contest. He challenged his constituents to write a speech for him. I'm always up for a challenge so I decided to give it a try.

I concentrated on trying to come up with a catchy phrase to begin the speech. I settled on "On the highway or the byway...." I won the contest and received a small monetary prize as well as a silver collector's coin with Senator Dunn's picture on it.

I didn't win a big prize but I gained the satisfaction of just knowing that I could do it. It was fun, and you never know when you might need a little help from your Senator.

> **You name the subject and there's probably an essay contest involving it.**
>
> *Have fun!*

*Circuit City Hero Essay Contest* I heard on the radio that Circuit City was sponsoring an essay contest to honor local heroes. The prize would be a $100 gift certificate from the store for the honored hero.

I felt that my daughter Diana deserved this one because of her recent heroic act. While driving to work one day she witnessed an accident; a car struck a motorcycle. Diana is a nurse. Immediately, and without regard for her own safety, she stopped her car and positioned it at an angle to protect the injured motorcyclist from being hit by on-coming traffic. She administered first-aid, and remained until the ambulance arrived. Her quick thinking and actions are credited with saving the man's life.

My essay won and Diana received the $100 gift certificate. She used it to purchase a new radio.

_Special Car Essay_   My teenage nephew Tony had a beautiful car, it was a custom purple color and it was very eye-catching. He affectionately called it "The Purple Monster". The automobile department at Wal-Mart sponsored an essay contest. You were to submit a photo of your car and tell why it is special in 100 words or less. I used the essay strategy of giving the title a catchy name, "The Purple Monster Car." My nephew won $50 for the essay.

## Cooking contests

It doesn't take any special skill to be a winner in cooking contests and they can be a lot of fun. Anyone who can cook has a chance to win and the prizes can be huge!

Cooking contests are often advertised in ladies magazines and tabloids. Of course you'll also find cooking contests advertised frequently in the "Best Food Day" section of your local newspaper. That's the day of the week when all of the grocery store ads come out. Here in St. Louis that's Wednesday, but I think it varies by local custom.

> _Anyone who can cook has a chance to win and the prizes can be huge!_

There's loads of information on the Internet about cooking contests. One site that I like to visit from time to time is www.recipecontests.com . You'll find enough cooking contest at this one Internet site alone to keep you in the kitchen a long, long time.

As of this writing there's a cooking contests underway sponsored by Mama Mary's Gourmet Pizza Crusts where the grand prize is a trip to Disney World and $5,000 cash. Not bad if you like pizza, and who doesn't.

Spice Island Seasonings is advertising a contest where the grand prize is $10,000. The runners-up in this contest win a gourmet gas grill with an approximate retail value of $1,400.

The grand prize in the Nestle Toll House "Share the Very Best" recipe contest that's currently advertised is $5,000. This contest tests your essay writing skills as well because the rules call for you to send in an essay telling the origin of the recipe and what it means to you and your family (100 words or less).

So you see there are many, many opportunities to participate in cooking contests no matter your tastes or your personal cooking style. Like the essay contests there's usually less competition then there is with sweepstakes, and the prizes can be very substantial indeed. Plus, you have the fun of brightening up your family meals as you try out various recipes.

Here's a few tips and guidelines that I use in my cooking contesting:

- Prepare your entry carefully. Make sure that you give the right measurements for the ingredients and the right cooking time.

- Be sure to use the sponsor's product in your recipe. This is a must!

- Use as few ingredients as possible. People are busy, they like recipes that are fast and easy to prepare.

- Use ingredients that are commonly found in most grocery stores. People don't want to be running around trying to find and exotic ingredient.

- Give your recipe a catchy name. Like "Fried pickle ice cream," or "Orange glazed pot roast."

- Test your recipe on your families and others. They might even have a suggestion for improvement.

- Be *creative*. There's that word again—the key to contesting!

- Be aware of current food fads, like the healthy cooking craze for instance. Study the magazines and newly published cookbooks to learn what the popular trends are.

- Last but not least, check your recipe over one more time before you mail it. Nothing can spoil your chances of winning quicker than having unclear or incorrect recipe instructions.

*Cherry pile baking contests*   I've won three cherry pie baking contests and my cherry pies aren't any better than anyone elses. My strategy for winning pie baking contests is simple. I find out exactly when the judging will take place, then I bake my pies about an hour or so before the judging. I take them to the contest piping hot. A hot pie just naturally tastes better than a cold pie.

*Cowgirl hat cookies*   Another strategy that I like to use for cooking contests, if the contest is an on-site competition, is to dress in costume to draw attention to myself and my recipe. For instance when I won a contest with my "Cowgirl Hat Cookies" I dressed in Western attire, complete with the cowgirl hat. I think that definitely helped me to win. When I participated in another on-site cooking contest with my "Fiesta Tacos" I dressed in a Mexican outfit. I even did an impromptu Mexican hat dance. This drew a lot of attention and my recipe won.

*Bar-B-Que sauce contest*   It peaked my interest when KMOX radio announced a bar-b-que sauce contest. In this contest my strategy was to use some unusual ingredients—soy sauce and mango juice. The contestants sent their recipes to the station and the judges selected ten recipes for a cook-off at the station's studios in downtown St. Louis. My recipe was selected and I went downtown for the competition. They had ten bar-b-que grills set-up on their outdoor patio. The station provided the meat (pork steaks), all I had to bring was my sauce.

While we grilled our meat the announcer interviewed us over the air. When he asked me why I thought my sauce was so good I told him that, "My bar-b-que sauce is so good you can marinate a brick!" I think the humorous comment helped me be selected as the winner. I won a smoker.

*Hidden Valley Potatoes*   You wouldn't think you could win a contest with plain old potatoes but my Hidden Valley potato recipe did just that!   When National Food Stores sponsored a cooking contest I submitted my potato recipe. The reason I thought the particular recipe might win is because of an unusual ingredient—Hidden Valley Ranch salad dressing. They notified me that I was selected as one of ten finalists in the cook-off to be held at one of their stores. They required me to prepare my potatoes on site. I won the contests and received $100 and a cookbook. As an added bonus they presented me with 100 printed index cards with my name and recipe on them. I included the index cards with my Christmas cards. My friends and relatives were delighted to receive my potato recipe and many of them prepared and served my Hidden Valley Potatoes for their Christmas dinner.

> *Nothing can spoil your chances of winning quicker than having unclear or incorrect recipe instructions.*

*Lorraine Cheese contest*   I spotted this one at a supermarket deli counter and immediately knew it was for me. I liked it because they were giving away more than one prize. The grand prize was a trip to Paris, but there were also first, second, third, and fourth prizes. This was a sandwich contest and I submitted several sandwich combinations, making sure to include Lorraine cheese. I used sauerkraut in one recipe, strawberries in another, and horseradish with cucumbers in another sandwich recipe. I was hoping to win the trip to Paris but I received a certified letter telling me that I'd won first prize; a bread-maker. My family enjoys the hot bread and rolls and pretzels that I prepare with it. To this day I don't know which sandwich won.

*Meat recipe contest*   When the meat department of a local grocery store advertised a contest for the best meat recipe I submitted my "Fire Alarm Meatloaf". My strategy was to give this spicy meatloaf recipe a catchy name and it worked. I won $100 and my recipe appeared in the store's flier that week, with my name printed under it.

## The Pillsbury Bake-Off

The Pillsbury Bake-Off Cooking Contest is a grand American tradition. The first contest was held in 1949 and the 2001 contest is the Bake-Off's 40th event. Contestants, both men and women, come from all across the country and from every walk of life, young and old alike. (You must be at least 10 years old to enter.)

The contest is now held every two years. It is probably the best known of all cooking contests and it has long been my dream to win it. It is such a splendid event that it merits the attention of every contesting enthusiast.

> *The Pillsbury Bake-Off is such a splendid event that it merits the attention of every contesting enthusiast!*

Just to be chosen as one of the 100 finalists in this contest is a fabulous prize in itself. Each of the 100 finalists wins a wonderful trip to the site of the competition, the 40th contest is being held in Orlando, Florida. The finalist trip includes three nights luxury accommodations, and $100 expense money. They also each receive a new GE oven. The approximate retail value of the trip is $3,500 and the approximate retail value of the oven is listed at $999.

The grand prize in this contest is $1,000,000! As if that weren't enough the grand prize winner also receives a complete new kitchen with all brand new GE appliances.

This year contestants compete for prizes in each of four recipe categories; Easy Weeknight Meals, Luscious & Lighter Main and Side Dishes, Fast & Fabulous Desserts & Treats, and Casual Snacks & Appetizers. Categories change from year to year. Specific category descriptions and instructions are included in the official rules. A winner is selected in each of the categories. One of the four category winners is selected as the grand prize winner while each of the other three category winners receive a cash prize of $10,000.

> **In addition to Pillsbury products there are eligible products from other Pillsbury affiliated companies including the Progresso, Green Giant, and Old El Paso brands.**

There are specific eligible products listed in the rules. In addition to Pillsbury products there are eligible products from other Pillsbury subsidiaries and affiliated companies including the Progresso, Green Giant, and Old El Paso brands. You can send in as many recipes as you like, but you have to complete a separate entry form for each recipe.

Here's how the judging process works.

The entries are sent to an independent judging agency either by mail or they may be submitted on-line using the Internet (www.bakeoff.com). This agency reviews each entry to make sure it complies with the rules, so be sure and dot your I's and cross your T's. They also eliminate entries that are judged to be too complicated or require unusual ingredients.

The entries that make it past the initial screening go to a test kitchen where the recipe is prepared and tested to make sure it works and works consistently. At this stage too, researchers search a library of cookbooks and food magazines to make sure that the recipe hasn't been previously published.

Recipes that make it through the test kitchen step in the process are submitted to taste-testing panels of consumers from around the country. The entries are judge and scored for both taste and ease of preparation. The scoring completed by these consumer focus groups determines the finalists in each category.

When the 100 finalist get together for the actual final judging they are given enough ingredients to make their recipe three times; one for the judges to sample, one photographic purposes. The third set of ingredients is provided just in case of a goof. The judges sample each recipe and select the winners. The recipes are judged for taste and appearance, consumer appeal, creativity, and appropriate use of eligible products. The judges themselves are experts in nutrition, cooking, and cuisine.

That's all there is to it. Sounds relatively simple doesn't it. I've been toying with the idea of entering my "Pickle Cake" recipe. What's a Pickle Cake, you ask? It starts with my applesauce cake recipe only instead of the applesauce I substitute pureed sweet pickles. I assure you it tastes much better then it sounds. I'm letting you in on my secret because I think it illustrates the kind of creative thinking that goes into winning a cooking contest, especially the revered Pillsbury Bake-off.

The Bake-Off web site lists some tips for coming up with ideas for your recipe entry. I think they are equally applicable to any other cooking contest that you might be going for.

- Experiment with new flavor combinations.

- Streamline a favorite recipe by combining preparation steps or making it more healthful.

- Create a new shape or appearance for a familiar food.

- Transform a main dish into an appetizer, or a dessert into a snack.

- Explore your own ethnic heritage for inspiration.

- Think back to foods from your childhood, then adapt them for today.

- Substitute convenience ingredients for several ingredients in an old recipe.

- Create a quick-and-easy version of a dish you've enjoyed at a restaurant.

## A Final Tip on Participation Contests

I'd just like to add one more tip about participation contests whether the winner is to be determined by a judge or judges. Anytime you enter a contest that's held in a store the judges will usually favor an entry from their town or area. The sponsors feel the contestant is more apt to be a regular customer of their business rather than someone who traveled from afar simply trying to win their prize. Unless the contest is a national contest, you have a better chance of winning if the contest is in your town or a close proximity.

## Chapter 8

# TV Game Shows. Your chance to be a star!

**In This Chapter**

➤ My appearance on *To Tell the Truth*
➤ *The Price is Right* try-out
➤ My daughter on *Wheel of Fortune*
➤ Game show contact information

If you like the idea of winning a lot of money you just might be interested in learning about TV game shows. Mindy Mitola of West Orange, New Jersey won $146,014 on Wheel of Fortune. Greg King of Glendale, California won $140,685 on the same show.

A fellow named Frank Spangenberg won $102,597 on Jeopardy. Another man named Jerome Vered won $96,801 on the show.

Dave Brownlee of Westlake Village, California won $183,562 on Hollywood Squares. John Latham, Brookline, Massachusetts, won $130,784 and two news cars on the show.

The mother load for winning money on TV is Who Wants To Be a Millionaire. Texan Ed Toutant won $1,860,000 on the show. Bernie Cullen, a Californian, won $1,000,000, as have several others. A man from Michigan named Kevin Olmstead walked away with a whopping $2,180,000.

> **Kevin Olmstead from Michigan won a whopping $2,180,000 on *Who Wants To Be a Millionaire***

Think for a moment about the possibilities—$2,180,000! How much different would your life be if you won $2,180,000? All you have to do is make a few phone calls, answer a few questions, and wham in a flash you are on easy street for the rest of your life.

It's not an impossible dream. It happens to people just like you every week. All it takes is enough gumption to give it a try. Even if you don't win big money being a contestant on a TV game show can be a once in a lifetime experience.

## My Appearance on To Tell the Truth

I didn't have to audition to be on the To Tell the Truth game show. They called me up and invited me to be on the show after reading an article about my contesting that appeared in *Good Housekeeping* magazine. (Yes, contesting can lead to other opportunities.)

When the lady from the show called me she explained that the producers were planning to put To Tell the Truth back on the air. It was a popular show years ago, and now they were planning to bring it back with a twist—in order to win the big prize I had to fool the studio audience in addition to the celebrity panel. They wanted me to appear on the very first show but I couldn't do it because I was booked on a trip to Alaska, so I was scheduled for a subsequent show.

They flew me to Burbank, California to tape the show at the NBC studios. I met with my teammates; two ladies that would be impersonating me as "Carol Shaffer the Contest Queen." They had already been preparing themselves by watching my instructional videos titled "Win Big" which reveals many of my secrets and know-how for winning contests and sweepstakes. (please see the order form in the back of this book)

We rehearsed for two days before the actual taping of the show. I was instructed by the producers to talk less, the two impostors were instructed to talk more and to try to sound like they knew what they were talking about. I had to sign an affidavit promising that I would tell the truth, and of course the impostors were required to lie. I found that I could tell the truth, but still give the impression that I was unsure of myself.

We won the grand prize—$10,000! The three of us split it. My share was $3,333.33 and boy did I have a ball doing the show.

## The Price is Right

The Price Is Right is the longest running game show in television, the show premiered in 1972. People just love watching Bob Barker inviting members of the studio audience to *come on down.*

My sister Jo Ann and I tried out for the game show. We weren't chosen, but I think I gained a little insight into the show. Contestants are chosen from the studio audience after a relatively brief screening process. The best way to get tickets is to write for them and request that they be mailed to you. Contact information follows in this chapter.

> *The Price Is Right* **is the longest running game show in television, the show premiered in 1972.**

The ticket does not guarantee admittance to the show. Seating is on a first-come, first-serve basis. Audience members, the potential contestants, are told to arrive before 7:30 in the morning. You are asked to fill out a name and address form that are used to produce your name tag that one wears on one's blouse or shirt. The interviewers engage you in a little small talk, then they ask you to walk a short distance.

That's right they want to watch you walk. I guess they want to see how you'll look when you come on down.

After this screening procedure you are dismissed and told what time to return for the show's taping later in the day. When the names are called you heart is in your throat. Naturally you want to be on the show because that's what you're there for. At the same time it's easy to feel a little stage fright when you know that you're going to be on national television.

As I said, neither Jo Ann or I were selected. We did notice though that several people with interesting T-shirts were chosen. The T-shirts were the kind that have witty sayings printed on them. That may be part of the trick to being chosen. Another thing I noticed was that one lady wearing a brightly colored hat got to be a contestant. In contesting it always pays to standout.

## Wheel of Fortune

Everyone's seen the Wheel of Fortune with Pat Sajak and Vanna White. Pat's been with the show since 1981 and Vanna joined him in 1982. Vanna is recognized in "The Guinness Book of World Records" as "Television's Most Frequent Clapper."

One year my daughter Donna and I thought it'd be great fun to try out for the show, we'd always been big fans of the show. We found out when and where auditions were to be held and planned a vacation trip to California to try out for the show.

When we got there we found there was a long line of people, probably a hundred or more. They lined us up at school desks in long rows to take a pencil and paper test. Every other row got a different test, so you couldn't look over at your neighbor's and cheat, not that we would even consider doing such a thing ourselves.

The test consisted of trying to solve a number of Wheel of Fortune type puzzles. There were three pages of puzzles and they were really hard! On many of the puzzles there was only one letter revealed, and that was it. The did tell you the category—person, place, thing, or whatever. We only had five minutes to complete the test.

Our instructions were to complete as many of the puzzles as we could. If we thought we knew a portion of the puzzle—like if you thought you knew the name of a state but you could not figure out the city—we were to solve that portion and go on to the next puzzle.

They told us that they expected us to solve at least eight puzzles correctly in order to advance to the next stage of the screening process. By the time we were finished with the test Donna knew that she at solved eight correctly, no doubt about it.

> **When they asked Donna to tell a little about herself she jumped up like a cheerleader and yelled,** *"I baked 10,000 cookies to get here!"*

Only ten people passed out of the one hundred that took the test. Unfortunately your author was one of those that did not pass. I was thrilled for Donna though because she did.

They called the ten semi-finalists, Donna included, into another room where they found a mock Wheel of Fortune set, complete with a smaller version of the big Wheel. In groups of three they played a mock game, with pretend money and pretend prizes. Donna did her best to appear enthusiastic because she knew that they were looking for people with exciting personalities.

There was also a brief interview of each prospective contestant and it's at this point where Donna thinks she won her spot on the show. Donna sat on the front row, she said that her knees were shaking but she wanted to standout. You know how on the show they always ask the contestants to tell a little bit about yourself? When they came to Donna and asked her to tell a little bit about herself she jumped up like a cheerleader, all bubbly and happy, and yelled, "I baked 10,000 cookies to get here!" Well that was a pretty unusual thing to say. People usually say, "Oh, I'm married and I have two kids." Well everybody's that, but how many people say, "I baked 10,000 cookies to get here!" Naturally they asked her to explain.

When Donna and I decided that we wanted to go to California to appear on a game show we had one little problem; we needed some way to finance the trip. Neither of us was working at the time so we decided we would raise money by selling cookies. Everybody told us we'd never make it. Well when someone says something like that to me there's no way that we weren't going to sell enough cookies. So we made cookies and went to craft shows and sold cookies, and we went around to nursing homes and sold cookies. We sold 10,000 cookies and that's how we got to California. Donna is convinced that telling our story to the producers is how she won her spot on the show.

The producers of the show point out that in any given year over one million people try out and only about 600 are selected as contestants. They try to strongly discourage people from spending any money whatsoever to try out for the show because the odds of being chosen to be on are so slim. That is no doubt good advice, but Donna beat the odds.

> **The producers of the show point out that in any given year over one million people try out for Wheel of Fortune and only about 600 are selected as contestants.**

Another way to try out for Wheel of Fortune is to watch for the Wheelmobile. That's what they call their van that visits cities around the country doing contestant searches. You can watch for a visit to your area on your local Wheel of Fortune station and save yourself the expense of a trip to Los Angeles.

Anyway, they cut the group of ten semi-finalists down to three and when they got to three that was it. Donna was one of the three selected. This whole process took us all day. It sounds short in the telling, but in reality it took all day.

By the time we returned to St. Louis there was already a letter in Donna's mailbox letting her know that she'd been selected as a contestant. They told her when to come back to Los Angeles and she and her husband started planning another vacation trip to California. You have to pay for the whole trip yourself. If you win you can deduct the cost of the trip against your winnings on your income taxes, but of course you don't know in advance if you are going to win anything or not.

When the time came for the taping Donna was told to report to the studio at seven in the morning and it was another all day process. They did not tape the show until 5:00 pm. In the meantime they went over everything the contestants need to know.

My own experience with game shows is similar. They are very precise about what they want you to do. They tell you to look here, you better not do this, you better not do that. It's really hard to be perky and spontaneous when you have so many instructions on your mind.

> **A TV show contestant has a lot to remember so *Be Prepared!***

They told Donna to bring three changes of clothing with her because they shoot three shows at a time, and of course they are shown on three different days. At that time you could be a winner for three days. I guess they don't want people to think that you sleep in your clothes.

When she arrived for the show they inspected her clothes to see if that's what they wanted her to wear. They checked her jewelry and accessories too, to make sure they were acceptable. Then they showed her around the studio, did her make-up, and ran through pages of rules and instructions.

Then they took her to the actual studio where the show was to be taped and they practiced games. They practiced their stage movements, they practiced the Wheel so they could see how it pulls. Then there were all kinds of mechanical things to be done, checking microphone, and checking the height of the contestant relative to the set and to the other contestants. They practiced with the microphone, "make sure you enunciate," they told everyone. "Clap up here, don't clap down here by the mike." There's just a multitude of instructions. As I said, it's an all day process and there was an awful lot to remember.

When the taping started at 5:00 PM Donna was seated in the audience with the other contestants. Donna's cousin and aunt, who live in California, came to see the show and she hadn't seen them in about fifteen years, but in strict accordance to the rules she couldn't say a thing to them, or even look at them. If she did, then she'd be out. Those were the rules.

Donna won a trip to Paris, France, that was the grand prize. She won a multitude of other things too. She won carpeting, and pots and pans. She won a wine rack. She won a kitchen range.

Back when she was on the show they showed you a showcase room and you shopped for your prizes from that. You had to pick from whatever was in the room. She had to spend every bit of that money, sometimes on things she didn't even want. She'd think to herself, "I don't want that." Well, she had to take it or she wouldn't get any of it. It's funny really.

Then there were the "Parting Gifts", you know, the items that you see advertised at the end of game shows. She got a tiny little boom box. She got some baby clothes, at the time she didn't have a baby but she kept it because she was planning to have more kids. She won a year's supply of spray starch. (I got all of that.) She had to pay the taxes on all that stuff too. I'll have a little bit to say about taxes in a later chapter.

They didn't send Donna gift certificates, they sent the actual stuff. It came in a 18-wheeler driven by a stubborn truck driver. He wouldn't unload it because of union rules. By the time she got her prizes she was six months pregnant, she couldn't unload it so she had to get her brother out of school.

The items arrived in big boxes and crates with strapping around them. Wheel of Fortune suggested that she open up the boxes and inspect the items for damage in shipment because once you

**100**

sign the bill of lading acknowledging receipt it's yours. So she had to open every box and look over the item and make sure it wasn't broken before she signed for it.

All in all they said that the estimated retail value of Donna's day at Wheel of Fortune was $8,000. It was quite an experience for Donna and for the whole family, and one we will never forget.

## Game Show Contact Information

They say that the longest journey begins with a single step. That's true when it comes to TV game shows and the first step is to investigate how to go about securing an appearance on a particular show.

In general, each show is looking for outgoing and enthusiastic people. There is usually some kind of test of the skill sets that the show requires, so if you can't spell to save you life you might not want to try out for the a game like Wheel of Fortune.

If you aren't selected for any particular show it might not have anything to do with you at all or anything that you did or said at the audition. They are looking for a good cross section of the population and they take into consideration the race, age, sex, and background and so on of those individuals who were previously selected whose names are already in their files waiting to appear on the show. If they already have a large enough pool of previously selected Eskimos on file, for instance, and you happen to be an Eskimo yourself, your chances of being picked that day would be reduced.

> In general, each show is looking for *outgoing* and *enthusiastic* people.

Here's the contact information for some of the more popular game shows. Good luck!

**Wheel of Fortune**   The Wheel conducts auditions in Los Angeles several times a year. Send a postcard to:

> "Wheel of Fortune" Contestant Auditions
> 10202 W. Washington Boulevard, Suite 5300
> Culver City, California 90232.

Print your name and phone number and the dates that you will be in Los Angeles and they will call you if they are conducting an audition during that time period.

You can also watch your local Wheel of Fortune TV station for an announcement that the roving "Wheelmobile" is schedule for a visit to your city.

More information about appearing on Wheel of Fortune is available on the web at http://wheel.station.sony.com/.

**Jeopardy!**   You must pass a very difficult 50 question test to be a contestant on Jeopardy. If you pass the test you will be given the opportunity, immediately following the test, to play a mock audition game.

Testing is held throughout the year at the Sony Pictures studios in Los Angeles. You may call 310-244-5367 to schedule an appointment for an audition. Testing is also held at various locations around the country from time to time. These occasions are announced on the Jeopardy broadcast.

The Jeopardy web address is http://jeopardy.station.sony.com/.

**The Weakest Link**   The Weakest Link publishes a schedule of when and where auditions for the show are to be held. If you think that you are smart enough to be on the show, and thick skinned enough to endure what ever abuse you might experience, you may call 818-840-7664 for audition information.

**Win Ben Stein's Money**  To try to grab a basket full of Ben Stein's money call 323-520-4236 for audition information.  You can also send them an e-mail requesting information at futility@futility.com.   Include your name, address, and day and evening phone numbers.

**Hollywood Squares**  If you'd like to whoop it up on Hollywood Squares you need to call 323-850-0707 to set up a contestant interview at the L. A. studios.  The interview begins with a written quiz consisting of twenty "agree" or "disagree" statements.  Those that pass the quiz will participate in a mock version of the show.

More information about the show is available on the web at http://www.hollywoodsquares.com/.

**The Price Is Right**    Contestants are selected from the studio audience.  Send a self-addressed, stamped envelope to:

>The Price is Right
>CBS Television City
>7800 Beverly Boulevard
>Los Angeles, California 90036

Enclose a note specifying the date you would like to attend. The tickets are free and you can request a maximum of ten. Admission to the studio is on a first-come, first-serve basis for those holding tickets. No ticket guarantees admission.

The web address is http://www.cbs.com/daytime/price/.

**To Tell the Truth**    If you have a good story or think you'd make a good impostor you may call the To Tell the Truth show at 818-260-5827.  The show's web site address is http://www.totellthetruth.tv/.

**Who Wants To Be a Millionaire**   The rewards for appearing on this show are so great that, if you're serious, I suggest you give the whole selection process considerable study.  You should read the show's official rules. You can find them on the show's web site (link through www.abc.com) or send a SASE to:

> Millionaire Rules
> 500 Park Avenue, 8th Floor
> New York, New York 10022

Good news if you live in Washington or Vermont—you may omit the return postage.

Millionaire selects their finalists in two ways. The Millionaire team is travels to several cities in search of new contestants. If they are coming to your area you can register for an audition. Watch your ABC station and the other local news media for an announcement of a visit.

You can also qualify by phone by participating in the qualifying phone round. The phones are open from time to time according to the sponsor's discretion. Watch for announcements about when the qualifying phone lines are open on the Millionaire broadcast and one abc.com. Call 800-433-8321 using a touch-tone phone. Players are limited to one call per player per day.

Those callers that correctly answer five questions are eligible for entry in a random drawing into the Phone Player Pool. The five questions are multi-part general knowledge questions designed to be of varying difficulty. Each question has four answers that must be placed in the correct order based on instructions given in the question. For example, "Place the following states in order going from East to West: 1. Ohio, 2. Illinois, 3. Utah, 4. Florida"

Players hear the question followed by the four answers and enter their response using their telephone keypad. There is a ten second time limit. If you correctly answer all five questions your will be asked to enter your telephone number so you can be reached for a qualifying phone call if you are randomly selected for Phone Player Pool and selected by the game sponsor as a finalist.

A Contest Period is defined as the five day period in the month that the phone game is available. Players are limited to one qualification per contest period for the random drawing.

Each Contest Period 500 players who correctly answer all five questions will be randomly selected and will be put into the Phone Player Pool from which the game sponsor, in it's sole discretion, shall select Finalists. Only the players who are randomly selected for the Phone Player Pool and selected by the game sponsor as a finalist will receive the qualifying phone call.

It's estimated that one hundred thousand players will compete in the phone contest on a given day, and that approximately four thousand calls per day will answer all five questions correctly. Doing the math then even if you answer all five questions correctly your name is still in a pool of 20,000 players from which 500 players names will be drawn for consideration.

It's all not as complicated as it sounds really, and it's fair. The sponsors take steps to ensure that access to the contest is equal, no matter what time zone or geographic location in which you live.

## Chapter 9

# You're Never Too Old, or Too Young!
## Contesting for Children

---

**In This Chapter**

➤ A kid's smile is a wonderful prize
➤ Representative contests for children
➤ Fun for the whole family

---

## A kid's smile is a wonderful prize

I get the biggest thrill when one of the children in my family win a contest or sweepstakes. Being able to include the whole family is one of the most rewarding things to me about the hobby of contesting. And a kid's smiles and giggles and general delight is one of the best prizes of all.

My ten-year-old grandson Ryan, and my twelve-year-old great niece Erika, are our latest winners among the younger members of the family. They each won the Nabisco/Kids Starting Line Up Sweepstakes sponsored by Shop N Save grocery stores. This was a mail-in sweepstakes open to residents of Illinois and Missouri aged five to twelve years old. You could only send in one entry per person, but nothing in the rules said that you couldn't send in one entry for each grandchild or niece. We dyed one entry blank red, drew a Cardinal bird on another, and glued a Cardinal cut-out on another. I don't know which of the ploys worked, but Ryan's and Erika's names were selected.

They each won four tickets to a St. Louis Cardinal baseball game. Better yet Ryan's game happened to be on Father's Day. He and his family had a great time at Bush Stadium. Ryan got to meet all of the players. He was paired with Cardinal second baseman Placido Polanco and got to go out on the field with him during warm ups.

> **Being able to include the whole family is one of the most rewarding things to me about the hobby of contesting.**

Ryan's name was flashed on the big scoreboard, along with the ball player's names. He was awarded a Cardinal shirt and ball cap and he and his whole family got to watch the game in a V. I. P. room, much to his delight. To top it off, the Cardinals won the game against the Chicago White Sox.

Erika won her tickets a couple of weeks later than Ryan. Her father is a friend of the TV cameraman that happened to be on duty at the stadium that day. He made a video keepsake for Erika of her "starting line-up" at the Cardinal game.

It just tickles me to death when one of youngsters in my family gets an opportunity for a special day like this. To me they're special kids and if anyone deserves V. I. P. treatment they do.

## A trip to Atlanta and the "Final Four"

My 13-year-old grandson, Jimmy, won the "Taco Bell Free Throw" contest to win a trip to Atlanta, Georgia including tickets to the "Final Four" basketball tournament. You could say that this was a sweepstakes/contest combination because names were first drawn in a sweepstakes and then the contestants competed in a free throw contest to win.

My daughter Donna, Jimmy's mom, spotted this contest in a Taco Bell restaurant and brought me some of the entry blanks. Six people in the St. Louis area would be chosen to compete in a basketball free throw contest at the Savis Center in St. Louis during the Missouri Valley Basketball Tournament. Jimmy was the youngest person chosen, but he won the free throw contest. He made two 3-point baskets and won the trip. Naturally the local newspaper did a story about Jimmy so a little celebrity accompanied his good fortune.

One interesting twist to this win is that we found out afterwards that Jimmy was competing with a broken arm. He had hurt his arm the day before in an athletic event, but he thought it was just a sprain. His mother took him to the doctor because the swelling in his arm wouldn't go down. The doctor said that his arm was broken and they put a cast on Jimmy's arm from the finger tips to the elbow.

## A Range of Choices

There are many opportunities out there for children to express their originality and talent in a variety of contests designed and promoted specifically for children. If you'll open your eyes and ears I'm sure you'll come across many contests that you and your children will enjoy participating in. Many of them are designed to be educational for the kids, but you don't have to spoil it for the kids by telling them that. Many, but not all, of the contests and sweepstakes for kids require parental approval.

> There are many opportunities out there for children to express their originality and talent!

I like to see the kids enter the kinds of contests that test their talents and skills. There are many poetry and essay contests, drawing and coloring contests, cooking contests, and contests that challenge the youngster's ingenuity.

My seven year old granddaughter, Hannah, won first place in such a contest that required her to use her creativity. It was the National Young Game Inventors Contest, a national contest held annually and sponsored by University Games. There were 700 entries in her age group. TGI Friday restaurants was a participating co-sponsor. The entry blank was on the back of the chains children's place mats. I brought one of the place mats home with me, thinking that "inventing a game," as called for by the contest, would be a fun project for when Hannah and her friend Jenny got to spend the night at my house.

An adult was allowed to help, but Hannah did most of the thinking herself. She used the strategy of "simplicity". Children tend to make their artwork too busy, so Hannah wisely decided that if her artwork was simple it would standout from the other entries.

She wanted to make a game about rainbows because she likes all of the colors, and she even called her game "The Rainbow Game." Hannah and Jenny cut squares of construction paper, all the colors of the rainbow, and glued the squares around the edge of an old game board. They covered the rest of the board with white paper then cut more squares to go in the middle of the board as drawing cards. When a player landed on one of the colored squares, that player would receive one of the squares of that color.

The object of the game is to be the first player to make a rainbow by acquiring all the necessary colors. Of course like any game there has to be obstacles. Hannah drew rainy clouds every so often on the board. If you landed on one of these rainy clouds you had to return one of your colored cards to the center of the board and lose that turn.

Hannah's creative mind won her a crate full of games from University Games. She also won a year's subscription to a children's magazine.

There are also many sweepstakes open to kids, and kids only, where the prizes have kid appeal. The people that make Barbie

Dolls, for instance, recently sponsored a sweepstakes for kids aged three to fourteen years where the prize was a special birthday party for the winner and 14 friends at participating Kmart restaurants nationwide. The party comes complete with a visit from Barbie herself!

The National Football League is offering the Staples Coach of the Week sweepstakes. Kids can enter on behalf of their school. A winning school is chosen each week and that schools receives a visit from the head coach of the local NFL team. There's also a chance for a school to win $5,000 in office and school supplies from Staples.

One of the best web sites devoted to kid's contesting is located at http://www.kidsdomain.com/kids/cont-more.html. You'll find links here to a number of kid oriented contests with prizes ranging from a year's supply of free ice cream, to computers, free trips to places like Disneyland and Washington D. C. The little contester can even win a little cash too. Funny thing about cash—it's a prize that appeals to people of all ages.

## Representative contests for kids

One thing about contesting is that there's always something new to grab your attention. The contest landscape is constantly changing. While that's part of the fun of the hobby it presents a challenge for me as an author. My research turns up dozens and dozens of contests for kids, however many of them have already concluded or are currently in progress and may or may not still be available for entry by the time this book reaches the reader's hands.

> *Many contests for kids are educational and a test of their creativity!*

I am listing a representative number of contests geared towards kids. A few of them are annual contests however most of them were, or are, one-time events. I think the list will still give you a good idea of what types of contests for children are out there, and hopefully get you thinking about what might be fun contest ideas for you and your family.

**Be Kind to Animals Kids Contest** When I heard about this one I thought what a wonderful family project it would be to enter and to try to win. It teaches the kids some big lessons whether they win or not, and if they do win the prize is very substantial.

For the last nine years the American Humane Association has sponsored the Be Kind to Animals Kids contest. This contest recognizes children age six through 13 who make a difference in the lives of animals. They fostered pets, volunteered at local shelters, raised money, and protected animals from harm.

The 2001 winner, 11-year old Shannon Watt from Maryland, won a $10,000 scholarship. She was selected for her community service campaign called "Vest-A-K9." Shannon's goal is to protect Maryland's police dogs by outfitting them with bulletproof vests. Doesn't that sound like a worthy cause! Shannon raised money by holding car washes, selling donuts, soliciting corporate support, as well as other fund raising activities. She devoted over 50 hours to her project and promises to continue until all Maryland police dogs are protected.

Additional prizes for the winner and runners-up include a $100 gift certificate for pet supplies, and assortment of children's books, t-shirts, bumper stickers, and special Be Kind to Animals merchandise. For more information about the contest call the Humane Association at 303-792-9900.

**Design-A-Tie Contest** Here's a fun contest for kids. The Golden Books publishing company sponsored a contest this year that calls for an original necktie design. I don't know whether it's an annual contest or not, or if they sponsor similar contests every year with various themes. I am including mention of it here because I think it's a good illustration of the types of contests and prizes that are available for kid contesting.

To enter kids age four to seventeen years old create and color an original design for SpongeBob SquarePants' tie on the official

**111**

entry form and mail it to the contest sponsor. The official entry form was available on the back of certain Golden Books and also on the contest's web site at www.goldenbooks.com.

> **One thing about contesting is that there's always something new to grab your attention!**

The entries were divided into two age categories for judging—four to twelve, and thirteen to seventeen. Judging is based on originality, use of color, and creativity.

The grand prize winner in each age category received a complete Gateway computer system, including a monitor and color printer. Five first place runner-ups in each age category received a Nintendo game with an approximate retail value of $200.

**Julie's Wolf Pack Wild Animal Writing Contest** This is a contest sponsored by HarperCollins children's books (10 East 53rd Street, New York, NY 10022). Children were invited to write a story of 200 words or less written from the point of view of their favorite animal. They are encouraged to include accurate details about the animal's habitat, food, and behavior.

The grand prize is a visit to the winner's school by famous author Jean Craighead George, author of *Julie's Wolf Pack* and numerous other children's books. The grand prize winner's classroom also receives $200 worth of Harper Trophy books.

**Toshiba ExploraVision** Here's an interesting contest, especially if you have an aspiring scientist in the family. ExploraVision is a competition for students of all interest, skill, and ability levels in grades K-12. The purpose of the competition is to encourage students to combine their imaginations with the tools of science to create and explore a vision of a future technology. This year is the contest's tenth year.

Kids work in teams of two, three, or four to simulate research and development teams in real world scientific work. Each team selects a technology, or an aspect of a technology, that's present in the home, school, or community. They may chose something as simple as a pencil, or as complicated as a computer. The kids examine what the technology does and how it works, and why it was invented. They must then predict what the technology may be like 20 years in the future and express their vision in a written description and five graphics simulating web pages.

Sound like fun? It sure does to me. You'll need a little help from a school teacher for this contest though. Each team must have a coach who teaches at one of the team member's school. The coach cannot be a team member's parent or guardian.

Judging is by four grade level divisions—primary, upper elementary, middle school, and high school. The judging is organized into six regional areas of the United States and Canada. The judging criteria is based on creativity, scientific accuracy, communication, and feasibility of vision. A judging committee selects 24 teams, one for each grade-level category in each of the six regions. A nation judging committee selects eight finalists teams from the 24 regional winners (four first-place and four-second-place), two from each grade-level entry category.

Student members of the four first-place teams each receive a U.S. EE Savings Bond worth $10,000 at maturity. Second-place winners receive U.S. EE series bonds worth $5,000 at maturity. That's certainly worth any student's time and trouble, not to mention the valuable knowledge to be gained by the participants.

For information about the Toshiba ExploraVision contest, call 1-800-EXPLOR9, e-mail: exploravision@nsta.org, or visit www.toshiba.com/tai/exploravision.

## Pillsbury Kid's Bake-Off Contest

As I stated in an earlier chapter, one of my dreams is to win the Pillsbury Bake-Off. I think the children in my family must have caught the Bake-Off bug from me. My grandson Jimmy entered his "Lemon Surprise Dessert" in the Pillsbury Kid's Bake-Off. My nieces

> One of my dreams is to win the Pillsbury Bake-Off. I think the children in my family must have caught the Bake-Off bug from me.

Erika and Emily entered their favorite recipes. Erika entered her "Gooey Butter Cake" recipe and Emily her "Fresh Fruit Crescent Dessert". Both of my nieces and my grandson got to participate in the local version of the Kid's Bake-Off. Jimmy's strategy was to use a Pillsbury product in a manner not normally used. He took Pillsbury Refrigerated Cookies and sliced them and pressed them in the bottom of a 9" x 13" pan to make a crust for his dessert. He then combined lemon pie pudding with colored marshmallows for a filling and spread Cool-whip over the cooled pudding. When Jimmy learned he was a finalist he practiced making his dessert over and over.

The Pillsbury Kid's Bake-Off is open to kids between the ages of nine and thirteen. Pillsbury partners with local grocers who sponsor the contest in their home towns. You won't find a Kid's Bake-Off in every state, however in the latest competition local contests were held in 33 locations where local retailers stepped forward to sponsor the competition. To find out whether or not a contest is to be held in your area you need to check their web site at www.kisbakeoff.com or watch for an announcement in your local newspaper.

Generally, the contestants for the local competitions are selected by a random drawing. The Grand Prize winner from each of the local contests advance to the National Finals.

Each winner of the local contests wins a trip for four to the National Finals and a GE Compact microwave oven and refrigerator. In 2001 the National Finals were held at Seaworld in Orlando, Florida. Eleven year old Christine Latta from Carmel, Indiana, the Grand Prize winner at the national level, won a $25,000 cash prize, and an additional $25,000 donation to the winner's charity of choice. The First Prize winner received $10,000 and a $10,000 matching charitable donation. Three Second Prize winners each receivee $5,000 and a $5,000 charitable match. All five of the top winners also received a GE Profile Advantium 120 Oven.

Unlike the grand old Pillsbury Bake-Off Contest itself the recipes for the kid's competition do not have to be original, although originality helps. The recipes are judged based on taste, appearance, ease of preparation, and creativity. The important thing to remember for children's cooking contests in general is to keep the recipe kid-friendly simple. You do have to use certain eligible products in your recipe so check the official rules.

## Fun for the whole family

Contesting is fun for our family whether we win or not, or whether the prize is big or small. It's provided us with many activities that we can enjoy together as a family.

My grandchildren love to color, so coloring contests appeal to them. I tell the kids to not only be neat and stay within the lines on their coloring contest entries but to also always draw a little something extra on the picture. We've found that the judges usually award a few extra points for creativity.

> *Contesting is fun for our family whether we win or not, or whether the prize is big or small.*

When my seven year old granddaughter Hannah won first place in a JC Penney's coloring contest the picture that she was supposed to color was a picture of Mickey Mouse with his arms outstretched. Hannah drew a line down from one of Mickey's hands and a circle—creating a yo-yo. She won a Penney's gift certificate in this contest. She's won several other coloring contests using the same technique.

The children in my family have won several poster coloring and window painting contests. I instruct them to draw big figures on their pictures, and make sure that their art work isn't too busy. The pictures should be like billboard advertising, simple and to the point.

As long as a child meets the age requirement for a contest his or her name can be entered in a drawing. Children can even help with some of the techniques I use to win. My grandchildren love

**115**

to help me decorate, especially with a bingo dobber, and/or draw pictures on entry blanks and envelopes. They also like to dip entry blanks in colored water to dye them. To the children it's like decorating Easter Eggs, only they don't have to wait for Easter.

Kids like stickers and love to apply them to entries and post cards. Sometimes they help me paste the stamps on the big colorful envelopes. In fact, just about anything that I do to decorate entries the kids can also do.

Contesting is a fun way to entertain the little ones. Here's a partial list of the loot that my grandchildren have won in drawings and contests:

| | |
|---|---|
| Amanda | 8-foot sock filled with toys and games |
| | Four concert tickets |
| | Children's video |
| | Personal alarm clock |
| | |
| Jimmy | 8-foot sock filled with toys and games |
| | Four concert tickets |
| | Baseball and bat set |
| | $50 bag of groceries |
| | Batman video |
| | Trip to Atlanta and the "Final Four" |
| | |
| Ryan | Baseball and bat set |
| | Personal alarm clock |
| | Camera |
| | Skateboard |
| | |
| Hannah | Sylvester the Cat stuffed animal, value $150 |
| | Personal alarm clock |
| | Camera |
| | Four Cardinal baseball tickets |
| | M & M stuffed toy |
| | Barbie dolls |
| | Muni Opera tickets |
| | |
| Alynn | Bugs Bunny Rabbit, value $150 |
| | |
| David | Go-cart |
| | $100 and birthday party supplies |
| | $100 savings bond |

**116**

## Chapter 10

# Contesting In the New Millennium!
## Making the Internet payoff

---

**In This Chapter**

➤ Contesting from the comfort of your home
➤ Pro's and con's of on-line contesting
➤ Virtumundo - success story based on fun
➤ Acuwin.com - automated sweepstakes entries
➤ ContestListings.com
➤ EZsweeps.com
➤ iWon.com - Internet portal web site

---

## Contesting from the comfort of your home

This chapter is dedicated to those of you who have mastered the computer world and feel comfortable navigating the World Wide Web. If you don't happen to fall into that category that is perfectly OK. The contesting world offers something for everybody!

The world of the Internet is such a fast paced, ever changing, environment that's not possible to be sure that any given web site made reference to in this book will still be functioning at the time you are reading this. That's unfortunate, but it's a fact of life on the Internet. On the other hand, it could be that the reader will find dozens of other new web sites that are even bigger and better than the ones mentioned here. My intention is merely to give you a quick look into the world of Internet contesting and I'm sure you can take it from there.

Once you take a peek into the world of contesting on-line you are going to be completely overwhelmed. There are so many opportunities it makes my head spin! All you have to do is spend a mere thirty minutes at your keyboard and you can find literally hundreds of contests and sweepstakes right at your fingertips.

Be careful though. If you are a truly dedicated contesting hobbyist you could find yourself glued to your computer day and night entering one sweepstakes after another. I suggest that you try to pace yourself, otherwise your family might be tempted to pull the plug on you.

## Pro's and con's of on-line contesting

Contesting on-line is fun, and best of all it's terrifically convenient, but like everything else in life it has its pro's and con's .

The obvious problem with on-line contesting is that it is so very easy to enter that you are almost always throwing your hat into a very, very crowded ring. Personally, I have more fun slipping my entry into a little noticed entry box at the local supermarket, where there might be a couple of hundred entries all together, rather than throwing my entry in on-line, amongst millions of others.

> **Many of the on-line entry contests and sweepstakes are geared to collecting personal information about you.**

Another thing to remember about the on-line entry game is that many of these contesting sites on the Internet are not strictly what they appear to be.

The sponsors of most traditional contests and sweepstakes are promoting their product or service. The purpose of the game is to get people to try their product, or come into their store. Many of the on-line entry contests and sweepstakes are geared to one thing—collecting personal information about you. I would even go so far as to say that is the purpose of the majority of them. They collect information that they can sell, or rent, to mass marketers who use it to target their commercial offers.

These sites sometimes ask a lot of questions. They want to know your age, your income, your favorite pastimes, how many kids, are you planning any major purchases in the near future, etc. Many people don't mind sharing this kind of information with strangers, but many people don't like it. It's a matter of personal preference, I suppose, but it's an aspect of on-line contesting that we all should be aware of. The information gathering capabilities made possible by computer technology is truly impressive. If you are one of those who don't like the idea of the corporate world knowing too much about you, you may wish to pass up on-line contesting completely.

## Virtumundo, Inc. An Internet success story that's based on Fun!

Virtumundo owns and operates two Internet gaming sites; TreeLoot.com, and CarHunt.com. Both of these sites are more like video games, really, than what you'd normally think of as a contest or sweepstakes. Virtumundo is a very successful company. The company offers prizes or merchandise credits for clicking through on advertisements or accepting e-mails and filling out an extensive personal information sheet. This data is where the company makes most of its money, by sharing the information with other companies at a price.

At the ultra popular TreeLoot site the player is guided by a playful monkey as he or she uses their mouse to click around in various places in the monkey's tree. The more you click, the more "Banana Bucks" you can win. Click in just the right place and you could end up winning as much as $25,000 in Banana Bucks. The player can earn additional Bucks by visiting advertiser's Internet sites, and/or by completing TreeLoot's registration and survey form giving them information about yourself and your interests.

Banana Bucks aren't too hard to come by on the TreeLoot site. In fact, I'd say it's down right easy to win something, but there's a reason for that. With some exceptions the Banana Bucks can only be redeemed as a discount on one of the advertised offers that appear on the prize redemption page. If you are in the market for the product, I suppose it's a good deal. You may find though, after you've played their game, that you don't find a prize that interests you. Even on those items that you can redeem outright with your Banana Bucks, you may be asked to pay a shipping and handling fee.

> **It's down right easy to win "Banana Bucks" at TreeLoot.com**

The CarHunt site is similar to TreeLoot only instead of searching for Banana Bucks by clicking tree limbs and leafs on the Monkey Tree one is searching for the keys to a brand new car by clicking at various spots on an illustration of the car. Find three keys, win the car. It sounds simple but I'm afraid it's a little harder to win then it sounds. The player is encouraged to visit the advertiser's web sites in order to earn bonus clicks and hints about where the car keys might be found.

Both sites, TreeLoot and CarHunt, are fun Internet addresses of interest to any contestor. They are colorful and they both have really cute graphics. I suggest you take a look for yourself. Be careful though, they are so much fun that they can be downright addictive. They can also drive a person a little bit crazy with the idea that with just one more click of the mouse you could be a winner. Make sure you have a little time to spend when you visit these sites, it can be hard to pull yourself away.

## Acuwin.com

Here's a novel approach to contesting. There is a service found at
www.acuwin.com. For a monthly membership fee of $14.95
Acuwin says that they will enter your name in thousands of
sweepstakes automatically. Once you become a member you will
begin being entered into sweepstakes all over the Internet.
Entries are made every day, and new sweepstakes are added all the
time.

According to their figures my name was entered in sweepstakes
more than 4,000 times in one month, with estimated total prize
value for all contests of over $8 million! Wow! I am constantly
searching for sweepstakes to enter, but I have never sent in
anything close to that many sweepstakes entries in just one
month.

Acuwin has an interesting "Member
Forum" section where people post
messages and exchange helpful
information. For instance, there's a
subsection of the Member Forum
titled "Tips and Hints" where
members post their best contesting
ideas. There's another subsection
titled "Prize Trading". The day I

> **Acuwin.com entered
> my name more than
> 4,000 times in one
> month, with prize
> value for all contests
> of over $8 million!**

looked one fellow had just won a contest where the prize was a
ride with Richard Petty in a NASCAR race-car at any track in the
country. Wouldn't that be a thrill for a real race fan! This fellow
was taking offers starting at $250.00 in cash or other prizes. Any
race fans out there?

There's a "Sweepstakes List" at Acuwin that posts a list of over
200 different sweepstakes and contests that may be entered on
line. Of these, Acuwin list's about half of them as "Auto" which
means that you will be automatically entered in these sweeps as a
paid-up member of Acuwin. About half of the remaining listing

sweeps are characterized as "Auto-fill" which means that you actually have to visit the contest's web site to enter the contest, but Acuwin's entry process helps you speed through completion of the entry form. Acuwin characterizes the remaining sweeps as "Manual", meaning you have to fill in all of the entry information yourself.

Is Acuwin worth the membership fee? I could not tell you. The answer to that question would vary from individual to individual depending on how much fun and enjoyment a person finds at the site, and how much extra money they have for contesting. I would say that it is one of the most unique contesting site that I've seen and one any on-line contester would enjoy taking a look at.

## ContestListings.Com

ContestListings.Com is a fairly handy source for both on-line and off-line contesting. That is if you can endure all of the pop up advertising that open on your browser when you click on a particular category on their site. Of course, pop up advertising is just part of the game whenever you are on-line.

ContestListings.Com lists links to other web sites under the following categories:

| | |
|---|---|
| Betting and Gambling | Freebie Directories |
| Contest Directories | Get Paid to Surf |
| Coupons and Savings | Knowledge and Trivia |
| Essay Contests | Online Lotto |
| Free Stuff | Play and Win |
| Surveys and Polls | Talent and Beauty |

Some of these links are contesting related, and some of them aren't . Betting and Gambling, for instance, is definitely not contesting in my book!

**Sears Essay Contest**

There are some gems to be found as you sift through the links. For instance, under the "Essay Contest" link I find that Sears is sponsoring a contest right now inviting folks to submit a humorous story about receiving a misfit gift that requires a trip to the return merchandise line. That's a cute idea for a contest. Who hasn't received a gift now and then that deserved to be promptly returned? Submissions may be made by e-mail—that's great, no stamps to buy. The grand prize in this contest is a $5,000 Sears Gift Card!

**$5 Million Dollar Birthday Game**

There's an interesting sweepstakes under the link category titled "Play and Win", it's called the "$5 Million Dollar Birthday Game" sponsored by EZsweeps.com. (More on Ezsweeps.com later.) All you have to do to enter is type in your gender, name and address and other contact information, and of course your birthday. If you can enter the contest everyday, if you want to, but you have to register with EZsweeps and return to the Ezsweeps web site to enter.

When the $5 Million Dollar Birthday Game comes to a close the winning birth date will be selected first; month, day, and year. Then the contest sponsors will select one valid entry from all of the entries submitted prior to the contest deadline. If the month on the selected entry matches the month of the predetermined winning birthday, the contestant will win $1,000. If both the month and day of birth on the selected entry exactly match the month and day of the predetermined winning birthday, the contestant will win $2,000. If the birthday (month, day and year) on the selected entry matches the predetermined winning birthday, the contestant will win the grand prize—$5 Million

> ContestListing.Com is a handy source for both on-line and off-line contesting.

payable as a forty year annuity or, at the option of the contest sponsor, a cash lump sum of $2,000,000.

Now that's a nice prize! The odds of being selected as the official finalist/contestant depend on the number of entries received. The odds of matching the predetermined winning birthday are one in 26,645.

### Rank-a-Person

Here's a contest that I thought was funny that I found under the "Sign Up and Win" link on ContestLising.com, it's called Rank a Person. Contestants are invited to look at pictures of everyday people and grade them on their looks. You get to rate these folks on a scale of one to ten and while you are at it it can sign up for a chance to win $25,000. You can even post your own picture if you want to, and get rated yourself.

You can choose to rank only the men, or only the women, or both if that's your style. Each time a picture is displayed, you enter your rating number from one to ten. You can then compare the number that you assigned with the average number entered by everybody who rated that picture. I don't know if you would exactly call it contesting, but it's fun and it's kind of interesting to see how your evaluation compares with everyone else's. It appears that the real purpose of this web site is matchmaking for those in seek of a member of the opposite sex. And there is that $25,000 sweepstakes to lure we dedicated contesters to the site. You can only enter the drawing once.

### Miss Internet 2000

If you are a beauty queen, or have a desire to be one, you might be interested in the "Miss Internet 2000" web site found under ContestListings.Com's "Talent and Beauty" category link. This is a beauty pageant for girls aged 18 to 30 offers monthly prizes of $5,000, $3,000, and $2,000. The grand prize for the winner of the annual final is $40,000. Participation is free, but I'll warn you that it looks complicated to me. I'm not even going to take a stab at explaining the rules.

**124**

If you're over 30, as some of us are, don't worry you're not completely out of luck. You'll also find "Lady Internet-2000" on ContestListings.Com. This is a free beauty pageant for intellectual, charming, and attractive females of above 30. The monthly and annual prizes for Lady Internet are the same as they are in the contest for the younger ladies.

# EZsweeps.com

EZsweeps.com is another gold mine for Internet contesting. Once you register by giving them your basic contact information you are presented with a veritable smorgasbord of on-line contests. On my first visit to this site I found a listing of 27 different on-line contests that I could enter immediately. As a contest hobbyist, my heart skipped a beat. Here's the list that was presented on this particular day:

| Prize | Sponsor |
|---|---|
| Internet Shopping Spree or $5,000 Cash | Discover Gold |
| $1,000, plus Bookspan Gift Pack | Lifetime Television |
| $100,000 Cash | Biogenesis.net |
| $25,000 Cash | BodyEq.Com |
| $25,000 Cash, 2002 Ford Mustang covertible or 2002 Chrysler  PT | MGMMirage.com |
| 2002 Chrysler Minivan, Ford Mustang or $18,500 Cash | Global Life |
| Trip to Ireland for 2/with walk-on movie role | MissJune |
| $5,000 Cash | GroupLotto |
| $1,000 Cash | MyFree.com |
| $1,000 Cash | SendAFriendAFunny.com |
| $1,000 Cash | CustomOffers |
| $1,000 Cash | TrimLife.com |
| $1,000 Cash | Merchant Central |
| $1,000 Cash | Body EQ.com |
| $800 Cash | InfoRocket |
| $800 Cash | MailSweeps |
| $500 Cash | BidBay Auctions |

**125**

| | |
|---|---|
| Compaq Presario Pentium 4 | WinFreeStuff |
| $1,000 Electronics Shopping Spree | easybuy2000.com |
| Trip to Orlando | Florida Vacation Store |
| $5,000 Weber Grill Package | ValuDesk |
| Free Home Electricity for One Year | energyOn.com |
| 5,000 Minute Sprint Calling Card | DialFreeCalls |
| Children's Shopping Spree | Parents & Kids |
| $1,000 Worth of Steaks | Omaha Steaks |
| Day Spa Gift Certificate | Dr. Scholl's |
| Orlando Trip for Four | Tempus Resorts |

To tell you the truth, I have never heard of most of the sponsoring organizations. I suppose that is a very good reason why they are sponsoring a contest. EZsweeps members also receive notification of contest and sweepstakes opportunities by e-mail.

## iWon.com

No discussion of contesting on-line would be complete without mention of iWon.com. U. S. News and World report magazine recently named iWon one of it's "Best on the Web" selections. iWon is what's called "a portal" in Internet lingo, like Yahoo, Alta Vista, and Lycos to name a few. A portal is a web site that is conveniently laid-out and intended to serve as an individual's gateway to the Internet. Portals offer sources of news and information, they provide their regular users the opportunity to join various interest groups, they usually offer their users a free e-mail address. Of course portals also offer a search engine that help people find relevant information of interest to them throughout the World Wide Web.

> iWin.com plans a $25 million giveaway for Tax Day 2002!

As a portal, iWon appears to be a good one. It ranks number one in terms of user satisfaction among all portals, according to an independent study conducted by a market research firm. Contesters may wish to choose to make iWon their home page, so that it comes up on the computer screen right from the beginning when they start their browser. iWon offers millions of dollars in sweepstakes to visitors. You rack up chances to win cash prizes every time you log on to surf the Web. What could be more perfect for us contesters?

You have to register with iWon in order to have a have a chance to win, of course. And advertisers will probably use your registration information to pound you with ads based on your age, gender, and interests. The payoff though for giving up your personal info is that almost every move you make on this site earns entries in daily, weekly, monthly, and sweepstakes. One lucky user wins $10,000 each weekday, and someone wins $100,000 each month. The site plans a $25 million giveaway for April 15, 2002; tax day.

There seems to be a little bit of contester in everybody because iWon is one of the biggest success stories on the Internet. It's one of the top ten sites based on average daily reach across the Internet and a top 5 site based on page views. It is number one in terms of repeat visitors and number two in terms of time spent per visitor per month. I don't know why anyone would be surprised by those figures. People just plain like winning money.

## Chapter 11

# Watching Your P's and Q's

## In This Chapter

➤ No purchase necessary!
➤ Publishers Clearing House speed bump
➤ Deceptive Mail Prevention & Enforcement Act
➤ Read and follow the rules
➤ Use your common sense
➤ Know the laws in your state
➤ The word we hate to hear: Taxes

## No Purchase Necessary!

There is one important point that every reader of this book should clearly understand. You **never** have to order a product or pay a fee to enter and win a sweepstakes. Don't be fooled by a sweepstakes promoter's promotional material. You always have an equal chance of winning whether or not you order. That is according to federal law and if a sweepstakes sponsor violates it they are in trouble.

Many people wonder why, if you don't have to buy anything to have an equal chance of winning, sweepstakes sponsors sometimes provide separate "yes" and "no" response envelopes for entries. These envelopes help the sponsor provide faster response service to those people who do wish to buy the product that they are promoting. The "no" response envelopes have an equal chance of winning.

## Publishers Clearing House - The Prize Patrol hits a speed bump

On June 26, 2001, Publishers Clearing House reached a $34 million settlement with twenty-six states. These states had alleged that Publishers Clearing House deceptive practices in its sweepstakes mailings. Under the agreement, Publishers Clearing House agreed to stop certain practices that these twenty-six states deemed deceptive. For example, in these twenty-six states at least, the company will no longer be writing "You are a winner!" on their mailings, they will also no longer be using simulated checks, or be telling folks on their entry mailings that the "Prize Patrol" is coming to their house. They've agreed to stop using phony and official looking stamps and seals on their entry forms with words such as "prize affidavit" or "official document". Their entry forms looks so "official", it seems, that many people got the impression that they had already won.

Publishers Clearing House attracted the attention of state authorities because many consumers complained that the mailings made them think they would have a better chance of winning if they ordered a magazine from the company. Under the settlement agreement, they are now required to provide notice of a person's chance of winning.

> On June 26, 2001, Publishers Clearing House reached a $34 million settlement agreement with twenty-six states.

Is Publishers Clearing House the worst practitioner ever of deceptive sweepstakesing practices? The answer to that question is a big fat NO! But they are certainly one of the most visible, and their case is certainly one of the most highly publicized. I reference the Publishers Clearing House case to point out the fact that you have to watch your P's and Q's as a contester and as a consumer. Just as there are sweepstakes and contest rules that we have to follow as contestants, there are rules that apply to the sponsors of sweepstakes and contests. Unfortunately, not every sponsor follows these rules. It is to your advantage to be able to easily spot those promoters who employ slip-shod or deceptive sweepstakes practices. You shouldn't be wasting your time or money with them.

## The Deceptive Mail Prevention and Enforcement Act

The Deceptive Mail Prevention and Enforcement Act went into effect April 12, 2000. It grants greater authority to the U. S. Postal Service to better protect the public against deceptive mailings. This law applies only to sweepstakes sent through the U. S. Mail, not to sweepstakes conducted on the Internet or telephone, unless the mail is involved.

Specifically, the law prohibits certain false representations in sweepstakes promotion including:

1) Telling a person that they are a winner, unless of course they actually have won;

2) Saying that you must order something in order to win, or that you must send in proof of a previous purchase, or that you have to make or purchase or you may not receive future sweepstakes mailings;

3) Including a fake check in the sweepstakes solicitation, unless it clearly indicates that the check has no cash value.

4) Using a seal, a name, or a term that might give one the impression that the sweeepstakes is somehow connected to the federal government.

The law requires that all disclosures must be clearly and conspicuously displayed and readily noticeable.

Another interesting aspect of the Act is that it gave consumers the right to stop receiving sweepstakes mailings. Imagine, while contest hobbyists are constantly on the lookout for contests to enter there are people out there who don't even want to receive the sweepstakes entries in their mailbox.

> **The law requires that all sweepstakes disclosures be clearly and conspicuously displayed and readily noticeable.**

Under the law, sweepstakes sponsors are required to provide a reasonable way to request that a name be removed from their list. If an individual requests in writing that their name be removed, they are suppose to refrain from sending an entry to that person for five years. If they fail to remove a name that person has a right to sue in small claims court.

## Read and follow the rules

There is a world of information in that small print. Simply by reading the rules you gain an edge over the competition because most people don't bother. I've read that as many as 25% of all sweepstakes entries are disqualified because the contestant did not follow the rules. You can also learn quite a bit about the sweepstakes and the sweepstakes sponsor's real intentions by reading the rules. If the rules are unclear or you can't understand them you might not want to enter the sweepstakes at all.

Here are the things that you should look for in the official rules. You should check for each item, both to make sure that your

**131**

entry conforms to the rules, and to make sure that everything appears to be on the up-and-up with the sweepstakes.

The rules should clearly state that no purchase is necessary for you to enter and win. You should see this both in the official rules and on the on the entry form.

The rules should clearly state the terms and conditions of the sweepstakes, and the eligibility requirements.

If you can use a postcard or other form of entry besides the official entry blank the rules should clearly say so.

> **If the rules are unclear or you can't understand them you might not want to enter the sweepstakes at all.**

The rules should tell you when the sweepstakes begins and ends. Must your entry be received by the stated ending date, or do they go by postmark?

There should be a complete description of all of the prizes including the estimated retail value of non-cash prizes. Can you opt for cash instead of merchandise prize? Does the winner of a cash prize receive all of the money all at once, or is it paid in installments?

The rules should include the estimated odds of winning for each prize.

The rules should describe the method by which winners will be selected.

You should be able to find the name and address of the sweepstakes sponsor in the official rules.

The rules should state when winners will be selected and notified.

If you happen to win, what are the sponsor's publicity rights regarding the use of your name?

The rules should state a mailing address where interested consumers may write to request a list of winners of prizes valued at more than $25.

## Use your common sense

As sure as we are winners, we still need to use a little common sense in evaluating sweepstakes and contests. There are a few simple questions to ask yourself before you invest any of your valuable time and money.

Have you ever heard of the sponsoring company? Is it a well know brand name? Read the name carefully. Disreputable operators may try to fool you by choosing a name that sounds familiar because it is similar to the name of a well know concern. We know that Holiday Inn is a well-established and reputable company. Watch out if the sweepstakes entry comes from Holiday's Inn however. That would be an obvious take-off on a well-known name, close but no cigar.

Can you understand the rules? Are you sure that you are eligible to win? Does the advertising state that there is no purchase necessary to win? Remember, that is the law. If there is no clear statement that no purchase is required one might question the ethics of the sweepstakes promoter.

> **Beware if you have to buy anything, or spend any money at all to claim your prize, or if you have to post a deposit, or pay any fees at all in advance.**

Make sure the prizes are things that you would like to win. For instance, if the prize is a year's supply of paper diapers and nobody in your family has a baby why would you waste your time trying to win?  Is there a cash option instead of accepting the prize?

Does the grand prize go to only one winner, or is it possible that the prize will have to be shared by more than one individual. Read the rules on this carefully.

How good are your chances, really, of winning anything of value. Check the information on the odds of winning included in the official rules.  Often you'll see that the odds of winning a particular prize are listed at 1:1, which means that everyone that enters will win that prize.  You can be sure that the "Genuine Diamond" prize that's listed with a 100% chance of winning is no more than a low value diamond chip that comes with some kind of solicitation to buy something else.

Premium promotions, also known as prize promotions, are often confused with sweepstakes by unwary consumers.  We've all received this type of confusing promotional offer. "Congratulations!" the mailing piece says, "You've won a fabulous trip to Florida!"  When you call to claim your "prize" you learn that you are required to pay a "processing fee" or a "redemption fee" which is actually more than the prize is worth.

Another technique often employed is that the mailing piece let's you know that you've won something, but you have to call a 900 number to find out just what the prize is.  As you know, you have to pay to make a 900 number call.

Time share and resort condominium sale promotions often send out mailers announcing that you've "won" a free stay at their property.  Read the fine print.  You are probably required to take a sales tour of the development in order to qualify for the free lodging.  There are usually income and/or age requirements, and if you are married, both spouses must attend.  This is not a fraudulent sales technique, as long as the terms of the offer are clear.  I've taken a few of these sales tours myself on occasion, in exchange for the free lodging offer.  I've encountered some fast talking high-pressure sales people on some occasions, but not always. And in fairness to the real estate promoter I have only visited resorts where I might have at least some interest in buying.

Use you common sense. If you have to buy anything, or spend any money at all to claim your prize, or if you have to post a deposit, or pay any fees at all in advance, it isn't a legitimate sweepstakes and you should exercise some judgment about responding to the offer.

## Know the laws in your state

The laws on contests and sweepstakes vary from state to state. It's a good idea to familiarize yourself with any local statutes.

In the official rules of many sweepstakes you'll find the words, "Void in Florida, New York, and Rhode Island". That's because these states have very specific registration requirements for sweepstakes promoters. Florida and New York require a sponsor to register and post a bond if the prize pool is over $5,000. Rhode Island requires registration if the prize pool is over $500.

Most states do allow promoters to charge an entry fee for skill contests. Skill contests are different from sweepstakes, because the winner is determined by skill, not chance. But skill contests that require a purchase or an entry fee fall under particular laws in many states including Arizona, Arkansas, California, Connecticut, Florida, Iowa, Minnesota, Maryland, New Mexico, and Vermont. For example in Iowa the entry form must post in prominent type, "You Must Pay $ To Compete For This Item."

> Prize categories that may be subject to additional state regulation include: dairy, gasoline, liquor, tobacco, animals, banks, and insurance.

Many states have sweepstakes and contesting laws related to specific industries. Certain types of sweepstakes may be void if it is illegal in your state. Some categories of prizes that may be subject to additional regulation in one state or another include dairy products, gasoline, liquor, tobacco, live animals, financial institutions, and insurance.

Since laws are constantly changing and vary from state to state, it's a good idea to become familiar with the laws in your state. An of course it's another reason to carefully read the fine print on the entry form to make sure that you are eligible to win.

## The word we all hate to hear: Taxes

If you win cash in a sweepstakes, contest, even on a game show the prize money counts as income and must be declared on you tax return. Do not enter a contest or sweepstakes involving a non-cash prize unless you can afford to pay the taxes on the prize. If you win a car or some other non-cash prize you will be sent a tax document from the sponsor giving the fair market value of the prize, this is the amount upon which you will pay tax. Sometimes you can sell a prize and pay the tax, however sometimes a prize, like a trip for instance, is non-transferable and consequently can not be sold. It is rare, but sometimes the sponsor of a contest or sweepstakes will pay the taxes. When I won a one-carat diamond necklace from National Food Stores, they paid the tax. Yippee! The LHS Chrysler car that w won was valued at $30,000 and we had to pay taxes of about $7,500 including federal and state income and sales taxes.

> Once you start winning sizable cash and non-cash prizes you'll need to get yourself a good accountant to help.

Once you start winning sizable cash and non-cash prizes you'll need to get yourself a good accountant to help you. (By all means do not rely on my tax advice, I'm certainly not a tax expert.) My accountant advises me to keep track of all of the money that I spend on my contesting hobby as a possible offset against my winnings. I tally up all of the money I spend on postage stamps, paper, envelopes, pencils, pens, and markers, index cards, stickers, address labels, paper clips, dictionaries, books about contesting, subscriptions to newsletters, bingo dobbers, magnifying glasses, and the like. It can add up over the course of a year and it may help you at tax time.

Another tax technique that you may be able to employ is to challenge the fair market value of the prize assigned by the contest sponsor. It is, after all, to the sponsor's benefit to assign a high value to the prize because it generates more interest in their sweepstakes. Often times, I really don't think they research it all that much. They are likely to use the manufacturer's "Suggested Retail Price", which is often a higher than what one could find with a little shopping. A sofa, for instance, may have a manufacturer's "Suggested Retail" of $3,000, but be readily available for $1,800 in furniture stores advertising "40% Off".

When my daughter appeared on the Wheel of Fortune TV show she won a rather lengthy list of non-cash prizes. She was able to document substantially lower retail prices for almost every item that she had won. The key word in that sentence is "document". If you are going to take the approach of reporting a lower value on your tax return than the value assigned by the contest sponsor you need to be sure that you are able to support your numbers with actual ads or other documents to support the lower value. Of course, you'll want to follow your own tax advisors guidance on everything related to taxes.

## Chapter 12

# Pageants, Powder, and Potpourri

## Be alert & imaginative, and be the winner!

---

### In This Chapter

➤ Ms. Illinois Senior American Pageant

➤ Make-over contests

➤ An "Extra" in the movies

➤ Who says, "You can't take it with you?"

➤ Don't get discouraged

---

I'm sure you have noticed by now that I don't view my contesting hobby as a get rich quick scheme. As a matter of fact, money has very little to do with what motivates me in my hobby. Don't get me wrong, money is always nice and I have been fortunate enough to acquire many of life's luxuries through my contesting that I otherwise would never have been able to afford, or at least that I would never have bought with my hard-earned money.

The greatest joy that I've gained in contesting has come through what I call "The Fun Adventure Prizes". I am talking about participation type prizes that require me to stretch my talents a little, give me an opportunity to experience life outside of the daily ho-hum routine, or enable me to rub elbows with celebrities. I've met Miss America, spent the day with Oprah, dined in expensive restaurants with professional athletes and movie stars, done TV commercials, and had a speaking part in a radio comedy skit. These are the kind of adventures that have, for me at least, are priceless. I am constantly on the lookout for opportunities to enjoy life as it was meant to be enjoyed—front and center, and with a big smile on my face.

## Ms. Illinois Senior American Classic Pageant

This is one contest that taught me a little humility. I saw an ad in my local newspaper that Governor Ryan of Illinois was looking for candidates, sixty years of age and older, for the Ms. Illinois Senior American Classic Women's Pageant. The ad caught my eye because the idea struck me as a different kind of challenge. I sent for an application.

The application was pretty extensive. I'd say it was almost an essay contest in itself. It asked for information about my special interests, hobbies, educational background, and my life view since reaching age sixty. It also asked me to answer the question, "What Would I Like To Be Remembered For?" In one section of the application I was asked to describe what my "Platform" would be if chosen Ms. Illinois Senior. My answer on the platform question was: "Continued Education for Senior Citizens."

There were three categories for judging the pageant participates; talent, evening gown presentation, and the answers given on the application form. I chose to perform a tap dance for the talent portion of the contest. I'd been a tap dancer as a child and I'd also recently completed an adult tap class at a local college. I hoped to gain a leg up on the competition by choosing tap dancing for the talent show. Tap dancing is a pretty strenuous activity, I thought I might be able to display a little more get-up-and-go than some of the other girls, since this was a competition for seniors. I already had a tap dancing costume that I'd worn the prior year when I had taught a tap dance routine to my bowling team. That's another story. There aren't many choreographed bowling teams out there, are there?

| The Ms. Illinois Senior American Classic Women's Pageant struck me as a different kind of challenge. |
|---|

For the gown presentation I designed a long white dress with silver buttons and a matching shawl. I figured that by designing and making my own gown I would demonstrate that I was both creative and sensibly frugal. I think the dress may have cost me twenty dollars to put together, silver buttons and all.

The pageant itself was a three-day affair held in Chicago. As suggested on the pageant application form, I recruited sponsorships from local businesses to help defray my travel expenses. I found that the local business community was very supportive of my effort, they donated all of the money that I needed to compete and represent our hometown.

I did not win the Ms. Illinois Senior title, but I did win the talent portion of the contest and I was awarded a beautiful crystal mantel clock. One of the judges told me that I did not win the contest because I did not belong to enough senior citizen organizations.

## Make-over contests

If you want to be chosen for a make-over contest it helps if you make up a little story—that's the secret—some kind of a problem that needs to be solved. My oldest daughter, Donna, had always worn her hair long. I had been suggesting to her that she cut it for some time, and I thought if the hair experts advised her to cut her hair she just might do it. I sent her photo to Channel 4 KMOV "Monday Morning Make-over." The story/problem that I wrote was that she had always worn her hair long but that she had just started wearing eye glasses and she needed a new look— hair and make-up—to go with her new glasses.

She was chosen and to my delight she let the experts give her a make-over. She appeared on KMOX-TV before and after. They cut her hair short, dyed her hair a reddish brown, waxed her eyebrows, and applied make-up. After the show she came by my workplace. She walked right by me but I did not recognize her. Her husband and friends all liked the "New Donna."

Donna's make-over was such a success that I decided to enter my youngest daughter, Diana, for a make-over as well. She also had long hair, and because she is a very busy person, I thought that fussing with her hair might require too much of her time. She was expecting her fourth child at

> **The secret to winning a make-over contest is to have a little story--some kind of problem that needs to be solved.**

the time, she worked part-time as a nurse, and she ran a "Creative Memories" business from her home. Her story/problem was easy—she didn't have the time to style her hair everyday so she needed a simple hair style to make her life a little easier. The story/problem worked and Diana was also chosen for a "Monday Morning Make-over." They cut her hair short and changed it to an auburn color. The experts demonstrated some easy make-up tips for busy people. She looked as cute as a button and her husband and kids loved her new look.

## An "Extra" in a movie

When I won the $10,000 shopping spree at the Plaza Frontenac shopping center I wondered where in the world I would ever go to wear such elegant sequined dresses, and dresses with big matching hats to boot.

One day I heard about a contest to win a part as an "extra" in the movie "King of the Hill" that was to be filmed in St. Louis. This was a movie based on the life of A. E. Hotchner, a famous writer and St. Louis resident during the depression era. I wanted an opportunity to see how a movie is made. What better way to learn than to actually be in the movie? I'd always been intrigued by the film industry. This movie was going to star Karen Allen, Elizabeth McGovern, Spalding Gray, and Jesse Bradford. I determined that I was going to try to be in the movie too!

> **I made sure that my photo would stand out!
> I wore an elegant dress and a huge matching hat.**

In order to enter I was suppose to mail in a full-length photograph of myself, along with my name, address, phone number, dress size, shoe size, and hat size. The request for my hat size caught my attention—maybe if I wore a hat in the photo it would be the gimmick I needed in order to be selected.

I made sure that my photo would stand out. I wore one of the elegant dresses from the shopping spree, a black and white striped dress, with a huge matching black and white striped hat. It worked! I won the part and it was as glamorous and interesting as I had hoped it would be. I also got paid for the work, work that I would have gladly done for free.

When the time came, I was invited to the premier of "King of the Hill" in St. Louis. I took my daughter, Donna along with me. She wore my black sequined dress and I wore a blue sapphire sequined dress. Boy, did we glitter! After the movie—which I thought was very good and deserved more recognition than it received—we attended the premier party. I met and spoke with Mr. A. J. Hotchner himself. He is a very interesting man.

Because I was an extra in "King of the Hill", my name is now in the database of the local casting director that cast the extras for movies that are filmed in St. Louis. When the made for TV movie, "A Will of Her Own", was filmed in St. Louis I got a call to work in this movie too. These were adventures that I will not forget and I would not have had the experience if it were not for my contesting hobby.

# Who says, "You can't take it with you?"

Now please don't think me morbid, but I entered one sweepstakes that some people might think is a little odd. On Memorial Day I went to Vahalla Cemetery in Belleville, Illinois where my folks are buried. At the gate, they were handing out a survey promotional form. Those who answered all of the survey questions were automatically entered in a sweepstakes. The prize is two burial plots at Vahalla!

I answered my questions using a bright red magic marker in order to draw attention to my entry. I also carry one of those in my purse just in case I come across a contest or sweepstakes. If I were to win this contest I think it would be the ultimate prize. Any true contester would without doubt rest most comfortably in the afterlife in a sweepstakes-won burial plot.

# Don't get discouraged!

If you employ the tips and techniques that I've shared with you in this book, are you going to win every contest and sweepstakes that you enter? Of course not, but you will win, and win consistently if you are alert, creative, and persistent.

I remember one contest that I particularly wanted to win. I heard about it on KMOX radio in St. Louis. The St. Louis Zoo was sponsoring a trip to Africa, escorted by zoo personnel. When I first heard about the contest I immediately drove to the zoo to check out my chances of winning.

> There are always more sweepstakes and contests out there, *with lots of fabulous prizes to win!*

The entry box at the zoo was a big, clear plastic container. All of the entries were clearly visible. The rules said that there was to be only one entry per person and that ten finalists would be chosen from all of the entries. One name of one of the ten finalists would be announced over KMOX radio and that person would have eleven minutes and twenty seconds to call the station and claim the trip. KMOX's call letters are 1120. If that person did not call, then the name of another one of the ten finalists would be announced the following day, and so forth, until a winner was designated.

The first day a woman's name was announced. I waited nervously by the radio for her to call and claim the prize, but she did not. The next day they announced a man's name, but he didn't respond either. Every time a finalist failed to call back and claim the prize I became more and more hopeful that I would be the one on my way to Africa.

On the third day they announced a man's name from Arnold, Missouri. He called the station in the allotted time to win the trip. I was very disappointed and envious, but I know there are always more sweepstakes and contests out there, with lots more fabulous prizes to win. You win some, and you lose some, and that is what I like about contesting as a hobby. It is an on-going, ever changing activity. You never know what tomorrow might bring. I wish you a hearty Good Luck!

**"WIN BIG! Secrets Steps to Winning Contests"**
**Volume 1**
**How to Win Contests and Sweepstakes**
**VHS VIDEOTAPE - $19.95**

Learn time-tested, proven techniques for increasing your
odds of winning contests and sweepstakes. This amazing
breakthrough system teaches you how to win cars, prizes
and vacations. Easy to learn video teaches you how
to win big!

**WIN BIG! Secrets Steps to Winning Contests**
**Volume 2**
**How to Win Cooking, Essay, and Radio Contests**
**VHS VIDEOTAPE - *Free with purchase of Vol. #1**

In this information-packed video, you'll discover
how to improve your odds of winning word contests,
radio call-in contests, cooking contests and much more.
Make your dreams come true by winning contests!

**"The WinGenuity System"**
**AUDIO CASSETTE - $7.95**

Tap into your inner creative abilities with The WinGenuity
System. This audio program is designed to teach
you exactly how to maximize your chances to be a
winner.

**HOW TO ORDER: Cut out and fill in the order form below. Enclose a check or money order.
Or you can pay with a Visa or Mastercard. Fill in the number, expiration date and sign.
Mail to: 3 Lochhaven Lane, Ballwin MO 63021. Or fax to (636) 230-9757. Please don't
send cash through the mail. Allow 2 - 3 weeks for delivery.**

✂

| | |
|---|---|
| Name (please print) | WIN BIG Video Vol. #1    19.95 |
| | WIN BIG Video Vol. #2    FREE |
| Street       Apt. No. | WinGenuity Audio: _____ |
| | Shipping & Handling    5.95 |
| City    State    Zip | Missouri Residents<br>add 6.025% Sales Tax _____ |
| | TOTAL _____ |
| Visa or M/C    Exp. | **Mail to:** |
| | **WIN BIG** |
| | **3 Lochhaven Lane** |
| Signature | **Ballwin, MO 63021-8020** |

Printed in the United States
1753SLVS00003B/373